Data Visualization with Python

Create Stunning Dashboards and Insight

THOMPSON CARTER

Table of Content

TABLE OF CONTENTS

INTRODUCTION

Data Visualization with Python

Data is the lifeblood of decision-making in today's world. Whether you are a researcher, a business analyst, a scientist, or an engineer, data is the cornerstone of every field. However, raw data—numbers, text, images, or other forms—doesn't speak for itself. For data to be truly valuable, it must be **understood** and **interpreted**. This is where **data visualization** comes into play.

Data visualization is more than just a way to display data—it's a powerful tool to help us **uncover insights**, **identify patterns**, and **make data-driven decisions**. By presenting complex datasets in an intuitive and visually appealing format, data visualization transforms raw data into stories that are easy to understand, interpret, and act upon. It enables people to quickly grasp difficult concepts and patterns, see correlations, and explore their data in ways that are often not possible through tables or numbers alone.

This book, **Data Visualization with Python**, is designed to guide you through the process of creating stunning and insightful visualizations with Python. Whether you are a beginner just starting with data visualization or an experienced data scientist looking to refine your skills, this book is structured to provide both foundational knowledge and advanced techniques to ensure you can effectively communicate your data.

Why Data Visualization Matters

In an era where data is being generated at unprecedented rates, the ability to extract actionable insights from this data is more important than ever. The role of **data visualization** in this process cannot be overstated. As data becomes more complex and voluminous, traditional methods of analysis can fall short. Visualizations offer a way to interactively explore data, allowing users to make sense of vast amounts of information in a short time.

Some key reasons why data visualization is essential include:

1. **Simplifying Complexity**: Data visualization helps to **simplify complex datasets** by turning them into

graphical representations, making it easier for individuals to spot trends, anomalies, and patterns.

2. **Enhancing Decision-Making**: Visualized data helps leaders and decision-makers see the bigger picture, identify key metrics, and make informed decisions based on current and past performance.

3. **Storytelling with Data**: Visualization isn't just about displaying numbers—it's about telling a **story**. Data visualizations can uncover insights, convey emotions, and provide clarity, all of which are essential for making data-driven decisions.

4. **Interactive Exploration**: With the rise of tools like **Plotly** and **Dash**, data visualization now offers interactive capabilities, allowing users to explore datasets in real time and tailor views to their specific needs.

This book is dedicated to **empowering you** to create visualizations that not only look professional but are meaningful and impactful. Whether you are looking to track business KPIs, analyze scientific data, visualize social media trends, or monitor IoT sensors, the tools and techniques we'll cover will enable you to turn raw data into visually appealing, insightful, and actionable content.

What You'll Learn

Throughout this book, we will explore several key concepts and tools that will help you master the art of data visualization with Python. From the basics of **Matplotlib** and **Seaborn** to interactive visualizations with **Plotly** and **Dash**, we will provide step-by-step guides and practical examples for you to apply directly to your projects.

Here's a breakdown of what you will learn:

- **Part 1: Introduction to Data Visualization**:
  - We'll start with the **fundamentals** of data visualization, explaining why it's crucial for understanding data and making decisions.
  - You'll learn how to use **Python libraries** like **Matplotlib**, **Seaborn**, and **Plotly** to create basic visualizations such as **line charts**, **bar charts**, and **histograms**.
- **Part 2: Essential Visualization Techniques**:
  - Dive deeper into visualizations specific to certain types of data, like **time-series data**, **categorical data**, and **geospatial data**.

16

- Learn how to create complex visualizations such as **heatmaps, choropleth maps**, and **interactive dashboards** that help you convey more detailed insights.

- **Part 3: Advanced Visualization Techniques**:
  - Explore advanced topics like **3D visualizations, animated charts**, and **multi-axis plots**.
  - Learn how to customize your plots for greater clarity, aesthetics, and impact.

- **Part 4: Data Visualization for Business Intelligence**:
  - Learn how to create visualizations tailored for **business decision-makers**, such as **sales performance dashboards**, **financial visualizations**, and **marketing campaign tracking**.

- **Part 5: Real-World Applications**:
  - Apply your skills to real-world scenarios, including **sports analytics**, **IoT sensor data visualization**, and **research data**.
  - Explore how interactive dashboards and real-time data monitoring can be implemented with **Dash**.

- **Part 6: Best Practices and Future Directions**:
  - Understand the **best practices** for creating effective and insightful visualizations, how to

avoid common pitfalls, and how to make sure your visualizations tell a compelling story.

o Get a glimpse of the **future of data visualization**, including trends like **AI-driven visualizations**, **machine learning integration**, and the growing role of **interactivity**.

Why Python for Data Visualization?

Python has become one of the most popular programming languages in the world, particularly in the fields of **data science** and **analytics**. Its versatility, simplicity, and the vast array of libraries available make it an ideal choice for **data visualization**. Some of the reasons why Python is the go-to language for creating visualizations include:

- **Rich Ecosystem of Libraries**: Python has several powerful libraries like **Matplotlib**, **Seaborn**, **Plotly**, and **Dash** that cater to different aspects of data visualization, from static charts to interactive dashboards and real-time data streams.

- **Flexibility**: Python's libraries allow for a high degree of customization, meaning you can tailor visualizations to your specific needs, whether you're building a **business dashboard**, a **scientific graph**, or a **web-based application**.

- **Ease of Use**: Python's syntax is easy to learn, which makes it accessible to both beginners and experienced developers. Libraries like **Matplotlib** and **Seaborn** are designed to be intuitive and user-friendly, allowing you to generate professional-looking charts with just a few lines of code.

- **Interactive Visualizations**: Libraries like **Plotly** and **Dash** allow for the creation of highly interactive visualizations that can be embedded in **web applications**, enabling users to explore the data dynamically.

- **Integration with Other Tools**: Python integrates seamlessly with **data analysis** tools like **Pandas** and **NumPy**, making it easy to manipulate and clean data before visualizing it.

How to Use This Book

This book is structured so that you can follow along with hands-on examples, starting from the basics and progressing to more complex topics. Each chapter includes:

- **Clear explanations** of key concepts and tools.
- **Step-by-step tutorials** for creating specific types of visualizations.
- **Practical examples** based on real-world scenarios.
- **Exercises and tips** to reinforce your learning and help you apply the techniques to your own projects.

We encourage you to work through the examples and experiment with the code provided. The more you practice, the more comfortable you'll become with creating your own data visualizations.

Who This Book is For

This book is designed for anyone interested in learning how to visualize data with Python. It is suitable for:

- **Beginners**: If you are new to data visualization and Python, this book will guide you through the basics and help you build a strong foundation.
- **Data Scientists**: If you are already familiar with data science concepts, this book will enhance your skills in visualizing data for clearer insights and better communication.

- **Business Analysts**: If you need to create visualizations to track business metrics or build decision-making dashboards, this book will help you master the tools and techniques used in the field.

- **Researchers**: If you're working with scientific or experimental data, this book will teach you how to create meaningful visualizations for hypothesis testing, simulations, and more.

In Conclusion

Whether you're working with **business data**, **scientific research**, or **real-time IoT sensor data**, this book will provide you with the tools, techniques, and knowledge to create visualizations that not only look stunning but also convey valuable insights. By the end of this book, you will have the skills to create interactive, dynamic, and informative visualizations that tell compelling data stories and help drive better decision-making.

Welcome to the world of data visualization with Python!

PART 1:

INTRODUCTION TO DATA VISUALIZATION

CHAPTER 1

The Importance of Data Visualization

1.1 Understanding the Role of Data Visualization in Decision-Making

In today's data-driven world, the ability to **visualize data** is more important than ever. Data visualization is the **art and science** of representing data through charts, graphs, and other visual tools, which help us **understand complex information** in a simple, digestible format.

Effective data visualization allows individuals and organizations to uncover patterns, trends, and insights that would otherwise remain hidden in raw data. By transforming **numbers and text** into **visual representations**, data visualization enables faster, more accurate decision-making.

Why is Data Visualization Crucial?

- **Simplifies Complex Data**: Large datasets can be difficult to interpret. Visuals break down data into **easily**

23

understandable formats, allowing for quicker comprehension.

- **Identifies Trends and Patterns**: Data visualization enables you to identify **trends**, **outliers**, and **patterns** over time, making it easier to make data-driven decisions.

- **Enhances Storytelling**: A good visualization is not just a chart or graph—it's a **story**. It can guide the viewer's attention to key insights and help **influence decisions**.

Real-World Application

- **Business**: CEOs and managers rely on **dashboards** that summarize key performance indicators (KPIs) in real-time, helping them make **strategic decisions** based on actionable insights.

- **Healthcare**: Medical professionals use **visualizations** to understand patient data, such as trends in blood pressure or heart rate over time, leading to **better diagnoses** and **treatment plans**.

- **Government**: Policymakers use **interactive visualizations** to display data on national issues, such as crime rates or economic growth, helping them make informed decisions about public policy.

- **Social Media**: Platforms like **Twitter** and **Facebook** leverage data visualization to analyze **user engagement** and provide advertisers with insights on target audiences.

1.2 Real-World Examples of Impactful Visualizations

1.2.1 Healthcare Data Visualization In healthcare, visualizations are used to represent the **spread of diseases**, the **efficacy of treatments**, and the **health of populations**. For example:

- **COVID-19 dashboards** provide real-time visualizations of cases, deaths, and vaccination rates across regions, helping governments and health organizations make timely, data-driven decisions.
- **Disease progression** graphs are used by doctors to track patient recovery rates, allowing for more accurate **prognoses**.

1.2.2 Business Intelligence Dashboards

- **Sales Performance Dashboards**: Companies use dashboards to monitor sales data, customer behaviors, and regional trends. This helps sales teams target the right customers, adjust their strategy, and track performance over time.
- **Google Analytics**: Businesses and marketers use Google Analytics to visualize website traffic, track user engagement, and measure the effectiveness of marketing campaigns.

1.2.3 Social Media Analytics Platforms like **Twitter** and **Instagram** provide users with visual representations of engagement metrics, such as likes, shares, and comments, allowing brands to measure **influencer impact** and **campaign success**.

- For instance, visualizations of **sentiment analysis** can show how the public perceives a brand or a particular product.

1.2.4 Economic and Government Data Government agencies and think tanks frequently use **infographics** and interactive visualizations to represent economic data, such as unemployment rates, GDP growth, or election results.

- **The New York Times** uses data visualization extensively to report on everything from **polling data** in elections to **economic trends** like unemployment.

1.3 Introduction to Popular Python Visualization Libraries

Python has a rich ecosystem of **data visualization libraries**, each suited to different use cases. In this book, we will primarily focus on the most popular ones: **Matplotlib, Seaborn, Plotly,** and **Dash.**

1.3.1 Matplotlib

- **Overview**: Matplotlib is one of the most widely-used Python libraries for creating **static, interactive,** and **animated visualizations**.
- **Strengths**: It is highly customizable and allows for the creation of a wide range of **visualization types**, such as line charts, bar graphs, and histograms.
- **Example**:

python

```
import matplotlib.pyplot as plt

# Simple line plot example
plt.plot([1, 2, 3, 4], [10, 20, 25, 30])
plt.title('Simple Line Plot')
plt.xlabel('X-Axis')
plt.ylabel('Y-Axis')
plt.show()
```

1.3.2 Seaborn

- **Overview**: Built on top of Matplotlib, Seaborn is a **statistical data visualization** library that makes it easier

27

to create beautiful and insightful charts, such as **heatmaps**, **box plots**, and **pair plots**.

- **Strengths**: Seaborn simplifies the creation of **complex visualizations** and integrates well with **Pandas DataFrames**.
- **Example**:

```python
import seaborn as sns
import matplotlib.pyplot as plt

# Example of a box plot with Seaborn
data = sns.load_dataset('tips')
sns.boxplot(x='day', y='total_bill', data=data)
plt.title('Box Plot of Total Bill by Day')
plt.show()
```

1.3.3 Plotly

- **Overview**: Plotly is an open-source library that excels in creating **interactive, web-based visualizations**. It allows for the creation of **dynamic dashboards** and supports a wide range of charts, including **3D plots**, **maps**, and **contour plots**.
- **Strengths**: Plotly provides a highly **interactive** experience, making it a great choice for **web-based dashboards** and **data exploration**.
- **Example**:

```python
python

import plotly.express as px

# Interactive scatter plot example with Plotly
df = px.data.iris()
fig    =    px.scatter(df,    x='sepal_width',
y='sepal_length', color='species')
fig.show()
```

1.3.4 Dash

- **Overview**: Dash is a framework built on top of Plotly that allows you to create **interactive web applications** for **data visualization**. Dash apps are **dynamic** and can be used for **real-time analytics** and visualizations.

- **Strengths**: Dash is ideal for building **customizable dashboards** that integrate with **real-time data**.

- **Example**:

```python
python

import dash
from dash import dcc, html
import plotly.express as px
import pandas as pd

# Initialize Dash App
app = dash.Dash(__name__)
```

```python
# Create sample figure
fig    =    px.scatter(df,    x='sepal_width',
y='sepal_length', color='species')

# Layout of the Dash app
app.layout = html.Div([
    html.H1("Iris Dataset Visualization"),
    dcc.Graph(figure=fig)
])

# Run the app
if __name__ == '__main__':
    app.run_server(debug=True)
```

1.4 Summary and Next Steps

In this chapter, we introduced the fundamental role of **data visualization** in making **data-driven decisions**. We explored **real-world examples** of how effective visualizations have **impacted** industries such as healthcare, business intelligence, and government. We also provided an overview of the **most popular Python visualization libraries**, including **Matplotlib, Seaborn, Plotly,** and **Dash**.

Next Chapter: Getting Started with Matplotlib

In the next chapter, we will dive deeper into **Matplotlib**, learning how to create basic plots and customizing them to suit your needs.

◆ **Key Takeaway**: Data visualization is not just about creating pretty pictures—it's about telling stories and uncovering insights that drive smarter, data-driven decisions. 🚀

CHAPTER 2

Getting Started with Matplotlib

2.1 Installing Matplotlib and Setting Up the Environment

Before we begin visualizing data with **Matplotlib**, we need to set up the environment. Matplotlib is a popular Python library used for creating **static, interactive**, and **animated visualizations**. It's the most widely used tool for **data plotting** and forms the foundation of many other visualization libraries like **Seaborn**.

1.1 Installing Matplotlib

If you don't have Matplotlib installed yet, you can do so using **pip**, Python's package manager. Run the following command in your terminal or command prompt:

```bash
bash
```

```
pip install matplotlib
```

Once the installation is complete, you can import the library in your Python scripts to start visualizing your data.

1.2 Setting Up the Jupyter Environment

For interactive and convenient plotting, **Jupyter Notebooks** is highly recommended. It allows you to run code snippets and visualize the output instantly. If you haven't set it up, install Jupyter with:

```bash
```

```bash
pip install notebook
```

To start a Jupyter notebook session, run the following command in your terminal:

```bash
```

```bash
jupyter notebook
```

This will open the notebook in your web browser, and you can start writing Python code and visualizations.

2.2 Understanding Matplotlib Basic Concepts and Syntax

Matplotlib is structured around the concept of **figures** and **axes**. Here's how they work:

33

- **Figure**: The overall container that holds all the elements of the plot. A figure can contain multiple **axes** (plots).
- **Axes**: The area where the data is plotted (the actual graph itself).
- **Axis**: The x and y lines that help define the scale of the axes.

2.2.1 Basic Plotting Syntax

Matplotlib plots are created with the `plt` object, which is the alias for `matplotlib.pyplot`. Here's the general syntax to create a plot:

python

```python
import matplotlib.pyplot as plt

# Create a figure and axis
fig, ax = plt.subplots()

# Plot data (e.g., a line plot)
ax.plot(x_data, y_data)

# Add labels and title
ax.set_xlabel('X-Axis Label')
ax.set_ylabel('Y-Axis Label')
ax.set_title('Title of the Plot')
```

34

```
# Display the plot
plt.show()
```

- `plt.subplots()`: Creates a **figure** and **axes**.
- `ax.plot()`: Plots the data on the **axes**.
- `plt.show()`: Displays the plot.

Matplotlib has **various functions** for different plot types (line plots, bar charts, histograms, etc.), which you can use to create different visualizations.

2.3 Creating Your First Plot: Line Charts, Bar Charts, and Histograms

2.3.1 Line Charts

Line charts are useful for showing trends over time or continuous data.

```python
python
```

```
import matplotlib.pyplot as plt

# Data
x = [1, 2, 3, 4, 5]
y = [1, 4, 9, 16, 25]
```

```python
# Create a figure and axis
plt.figure(figsize=(8, 6))

# Plot a line chart
plt.plot(x, y, label='y = x^2', color='b',
marker='o')

# Add title and labels
plt.title('Line Chart: y = x^2')
plt.xlabel('X-Axis')
plt.ylabel('Y-Axis')

# Display legend
plt.legend()

# Show the plot
plt.show()
```

◆ **Explanation**:

- `plt.plot(x, y)`: Creates a **line plot** with data points x and y.
- `color='b'`: Specifies the line color (blue in this case).
- `marker='o'`: Adds circle markers at each data point.

2.3.2 Bar Charts

Bar charts are useful when comparing quantities across different categories.

python

```python
# Data
categories = ['A', 'B', 'C', 'D', 'E']
values = [3, 7, 2, 5, 8]

# Create a bar chart
plt.bar(categories, values, color='green')

# Add title and labels
plt.title('Bar Chart: Category vs Value')
plt.xlabel('Categories')
plt.ylabel('Values')

# Show the plot
plt.show()
```

♦ **Explanation**:

- `plt.bar(categories, values)`: Creates a **bar chart** with `categories` on the x-axis and `values` on the y-axis.
- `color='green'`: Specifies the bar color (green in this case).

37

2.3.3 Histograms

Histograms are used to visualize the distribution of numerical data by grouping data into bins.

```python
import numpy as np

# Generate random data
data = np.random.randn(1000)

# Create a histogram
plt.hist(data,      bins=30,      color='orange',
edgecolor='black')

# Add title and labels
plt.title('Histogram: Distribution of Data')
plt.xlabel('Value')
plt.ylabel('Frequency')

# Show the plot
plt.show()
```

◆ **Explanation**:

- `plt.hist(data,   bins=30)`: Creates a **histogram** with the data and divides it into 30 **bins**.

38

- `color='orange'`: Specifies the color of the histogram bars (orange in this case).
- `edgecolor='black'`: Adds a black outline to each bin.

2.4 Summary and Next Steps

In this chapter, we have covered:

- How to **install and set up Matplotlib** in your environment.
- The basic structure of a **Matplotlib plot**, including the concept of **figures** and **axes**.
- How to create **line charts**, **bar charts**, and **histograms** to visualize different types of data.

Next Chapter: Exploring Seaborn for Beautiful Statistical Plots

In the next chapter, we will dive into **Seaborn**, a Python library built on top of Matplotlib, to explore how it simplifies creating **statistical plots** and **visualizing complex data**.

◆ **Key Takeaway**: **Matplotlib** is a versatile tool for creating static plots in Python. By learning the basics of plotting with Matplotlib, you can start exploring and presenting data in a clear, visual format. 🚀

CHAPTER 3

Seaborn: Making Beautiful Statistical Plots

3.1 Introduction to Seaborn and Its Advantages Over Matplotlib

Seaborn is a Python library built on top of **Matplotlib** that provides a high-level interface for creating **beautiful, informative statistical plots**. While **Matplotlib** is incredibly powerful and flexible, it often requires more code and manual adjustments to create polished visualizations. **Seaborn** streamlines this process, offering a **more intuitive syntax** and **built-in themes** to create **aesthetically pleasing** plots quickly.

Why Use Seaborn Over Matplotlib?

- **Higher-Level Interface**: Seaborn makes it easier to generate **complex visualizations** with less code compared to Matplotlib.
- **Built-in Themes**: Seaborn comes with **default themes** and color palettes, making your plots look professional right out of the box.

41

- **Statistical Plotting**: Seaborn simplifies the creation of statistical plots like **box plots, violin plots**, and **heatmaps**. These types of plots are particularly useful for visualizing the distribution of data, relationships between variables, and correlations.
- **Integration with Pandas**: Seaborn integrates seamlessly with **Pandas DataFrames**, making it easy to visualize data directly from your data structures.

Installing Seaborn

If Seaborn is not already installed, you can install it via pip:

```bash
bash
```

```bash
pip install seaborn
```

Once installed, you can import it like this:

```python
python
```

```python
import seaborn as sns
import matplotlib.pyplot as plt
```

3.2 Creating Statistical Plots: Box Plots, Violin Plots, and Heatmaps

3.2.1 Box Plots

Box plots are used to display the **distribution** of a dataset based on **five summary statistics**: minimum, first quartile (Q1), median (Q2), third quartile (Q3), and maximum. They are great for visualizing the spread and skewness of data and identifying outliers.

```python
import seaborn as sns
import matplotlib.pyplot as plt

# Load an example dataset
df = sns.load_dataset('tips')

# Create a box plot of total bill by day
sns.boxplot(x='day', y='total_bill', data=df,
palette='coolwarm')

# Add title and labels
plt.title('Box Plot: Total Bill by Day')
plt.xlabel('Day of the Week')
plt.ylabel('Total Bill ($)')

# Show the plot
plt.show()
```

◆ Explanation:

- `sns.boxplot()`: Creates a **box plot** with the x and y variables.
- `palette='coolwarm'`: Specifies a color palette for visual appeal.
- **Key Insight**: Box plots allow you to quickly see the **distribution of values** and identify **outliers**.

3.2.2 Violin Plots

Violin plots are similar to box plots, but they also show the **density distribution** of the data, providing a deeper understanding of the **data distribution**. They combine aspects of a **box plot** and **kernel density plot**.

python

```python
# Create a violin plot of total bill by day
sns.violinplot(x='day', y='total_bill', data=df,
palette='muted')

# Add title and labels
plt.title('Violin Plot: Total Bill by Day')
plt.xlabel('Day of the Week')
plt.ylabel('Total Bill ($)')
```

44

```
# Show the plot
plt.show()
```

◆ Explanation:

- `sns.violinplot()`: Creates a **violin plot** to visualize the distribution of `total_bill` by `day`.
- The **width of the violin** at different y-values represents the **density** of the data at that level.
- **Key Insight**: Violin plots help visualize the **density and distribution** of data in addition to the **spread**.

3.2.3 Heatmaps

Heatmaps are used to represent **matrix-like data** in a color-coded format. They are particularly useful for showing **correlation matrices** or any dataset where the relationship between two variables is the focus.

python

```
# Load a correlation matrix of the 'tips' dataset
corr_matrix = df.corr()

# Create a heatmap of the correlation matrix
sns.heatmap(corr_matrix,                annot=True,
cmap='coolwarm', fmt='.2f', linewidths=0.5)
```

45

```
# Add title
plt.title('Heatmap: Correlation Matrix')

# Show the plot
plt.show()
```

◆ **Explanation**:

- `sns.heatmap()`: Creates a **heatmap** from the correlation matrix of the `tips` dataset.
- `annot=True`: Annotates each cell with the correlation coefficient.
- `cmap='coolwarm'`: Specifies the color map for the heatmap.
- **Key Insight**: Heatmaps are great for identifying **strong relationships** between variables and visualizing **patterns** in complex datasets.

3.3 Customizing Visualizations for Clarity and Aesthetics

Seaborn provides various ways to **customize your plots** for clarity and aesthetics. Here are a few common techniques to enhance the visual appeal and interpretability of your plots.

3.3.1 Using Color Palettes

Seaborn offers a wide range of **color palettes** to make your plots more aesthetically pleasing and informative. You can choose a **pre-defined palette** or create your own.

```python
python

# Set a color palette
sns.set_palette('pastel')

# Create a bar plot
sns.barplot(x='day', y='total_bill', data=df)

# Show the plot
plt.show()
```

◆ **Explanation**:

- `sns.set_palette('pastel')`: Sets a soft, pastel color palette for the plot.
- **Key Insight**: Choosing the right color palette can make your plot more **appealing** and easier to understand.

3.3.2 Adding Titles, Axis Labels, and Legends

To make your plots **more informative**, you can add **titles**, **axis labels**, and **legends** to highlight key insights.

```python
# Create a scatter plot
sns.scatterplot(x='total_bill',         y='tip',
data=df)

# Add title and labels
plt.title('Scatter Plot: Total Bill vs. Tip')
plt.xlabel('Total Bill ($)')
plt.ylabel('Tip ($)')

# Show the plot
plt.show()
```

◆ **Explanation**:

- `plt.title()`, `plt.xlabel()`, and `plt.ylabel()`: Add informative **titles** and **labels** to the plot.
- **Key Insight**: Clear titles and axis labels are essential for **understanding the context** of the data.

3.3.3 Customizing Axes and Gridlines

You can further customize your plots by adjusting the **axes limits** and adding **gridlines** for better readability.

```python
python

# Create a line plot
sns.lineplot(x='total_bill', y='tip', data=df)

# Customize axes
plt.xlim(10, 50)   # Set x-axis limits
plt.ylim(0, 12)    # Set y-axis limits

# Add gridlines
plt.grid(True)

# Show the plot
plt.show()
```

◆ **Explanation**:

- `plt.xlim()` and `plt.ylim()`: Set **limits** for the axes to focus on specific data ranges.
- `plt.grid(True)`: Adds **gridlines** to make the plot easier to interpret.

- **Key Insight**: Customizing the axes and gridlines helps focus on **relevant data points** and improves **visual clarity**.

3.4 Summary and Next Steps

In this chapter, we have:

- Explored **Seaborn**, a powerful library for creating **beautiful statistical plots**.
- Created **box plots**, **violin plots**, and **heatmaps** to visualize different types of data.
- Learned how to **customize** visualizations with **color palettes**, **titles**, **axis labels**, and **gridlines** for better **clarity** and **aesthetics**.

Next Chapter: Plotly for Interactive Data Visualizations

In the next chapter, we will introduce **Plotly**, an interactive visualization library, and learn how to create **dynamic, web-based plots** and **dashboards** that engage your audience and provide deeper insights into your data.

◆ **Key Takeaway**: Seaborn makes creating **beautiful, statistical plots** easy with its high-level syntax, color palettes, and integration with **Pandas** DataFrames. Use it to quickly create **insightful visualizations** that convey the story behind your data. 🚀

CHAPTER 4

Plotly: Interactive Visualizations for the Web

4.1 Introduction to Plotly and Its Capabilities for Interactive Charts

Plotly is a powerful, open-source Python library for creating **interactive visualizations**. Unlike static charts created with libraries like Matplotlib and Seaborn, Plotly allows users to **explore data dynamically**, making it ideal for **web-based applications**, **dashboards**, and **data analysis**.

With Plotly, you can create a wide range of interactive charts, from basic line and bar charts to more complex visualizations like **3D scatter plots** and **maps**. The interactive features—such as **zooming, hovering**, and **filtering**—make it a valuable tool for users who need to engage deeply with data.

Why Use Plotly for Interactive Visualizations?

- **Highly Interactive**: Plotly charts are interactive by default. Viewers can **zoom, pan**, and **hover** over data points to get additional information.
- **Rich Customization**: Plotly offers a rich set of customization options, allowing you to adjust **colors, labels, legends**, and more.
- **Web Integration**: Plotly visualizations are designed to be embedded in **web applications** and are supported by **Dash**, a framework for building interactive web dashboards.
- **Versatility**: You can create a wide range of chart types, from **scatter plots** and **line charts** to more complex plots like **contour plots, bubble charts**, and **3D visualizations**.

To get started with Plotly, first install it using:

```bash

pip install plotly
```

4.2 Creating Interactive Plots: Scatter Plots, Bar Plots, and More

4.2.1 Scatter Plots

Scatter plots are commonly used to visualize the **relationship** between two continuous variables. Plotly makes it simple to create **interactive scatter plots** where users can hover over data points to see the exact values.

```python
import plotly.express as px

# Load the Iris dataset
df = px.data.iris()

# Create an interactive scatter plot
fig = px.scatter(df, x='sepal_width',
y='sepal_length', color='species',
                title='Interactive Scatter Plot
of Sepal Width vs Sepal Length')

# Show the plot
fig.show()
```

✦ Explanation:

- `px.scatter()`: Creates an **interactive scatter plot**.
- `color='species'`: Colors the data points based on the species.

- `title`: Adds a **title** to the plot.

Interactive Features:

- **Hover**: Hover over any point to see the values of `sepal_width` and `sepal_length`.
- **Zooming**: Zoom in and out on the plot to explore data at different scales.

4.2.2 Bar Plots

Bar charts are often used to display the **distribution** of categorical variables or compare different groups. Plotly makes it easy to create **interactive bar charts** that allow for **dynamic exploration** of data.

python

```
# Create an interactive bar plot
fig = px.bar(df, x='species', y='sepal_length',
color='species',
            title='Interactive  Bar  Plot  of
Sepal Length by Species')

# Show the plot
fig.show()
```

◆ **Explanation**:

- `px.bar()`: Creates a **bar chart** where the x-axis represents the `species` and the y-axis represents the `sepal_length`.
- **Color**: Different species are represented by different colors.

Interactive Features:

- **Hover**: Hover over the bars to view the exact values of `sepal_length` for each species.
- **Zoom**: Zoom in on specific areas of the bar chart for more detailed exploration.

4.2.3 Line Plots

Line plots are typically used to visualize trends over time or continuous data. Plotly can create interactive **line plots** that allow users to examine trends and interact with the data.

python

```python
# Create an interactive line plot of sepal length
over time
fig    =    px.line(df,    x='sepal_width',
y='sepal_length', color='species',
```

```
                title='Interactive    Line    Plot:
Sepal Width vs Sepal Length')

# Show the plot
fig.show()
```

◆ Explanation:

- `px.line()`: Creates an **interactive line plot**.
- The **interactive features** of Plotly, such as **zooming** and **hovering**, allow for deeper exploration of trends.

4.3 Customizing Plotly Charts for Advanced Interactivity

Plotly allows you to customize your charts in a variety of ways, from changing **colors** and **labels** to adding **interactive widgets** for real-time exploration.

4.3.1 Customizing the Layout and Style

You can customize the layout of your Plotly chart to change the **size**, **axes**, **gridlines**, and more. This helps improve the clarity and aesthetics of your plots.

```
python
```

```
# Customize layout for the scatter plot
fig.update_layout(
    title='Customized Interactive Scatter Plot',
    xaxis_title='Sepal Width',
    yaxis_title='Sepal Length',
    plot_bgcolor='lightgray',          #     Change
background color
    paper_bgcolor='lightblue',   # Change paper
background color
)

# Show the plot
fig.show()
```

◆ Explanation:

- `update_layout()`: Customizes various properties of the plot.
- `plot_bgcolor` and `paper_bgcolor`: Change the background colors of the plot area and the surrounding area, respectively.

4.3.2 Adding Interactive Elements

Plotly allows you to add interactive elements like **dropdown menus**, **sliders**, and **buttons** to your plots. These widgets make it possible to **filter data** or **change the view dynamically**.

```python
# Create a line plot with a dropdown menu to
select different species
fig      =      px.line(df,     x='sepal_width',
y='sepal_length', color='species',
            title='Interactive Line Plot with
Dropdown Menu')

# Add a dropdown for species selection
fig.update_layout(
    updatemenus=[{
        'buttons': [
            {'label':     'Setosa',     'method':
'update', 'args': [{'visible': [True, False,
False]}]},
            {'label':   'Versicolor',   'method':
'update', 'args': [{'visible': [False, True,
False]}]},
            {'label':    'Virginica',   'method':
'update', 'args': [{'visible': [False, False,
True]}]},
        ],
        'direction': 'down',
        'showactive': True,
    }]
```

```
)
```

```
# Show the plot
fig.show()
```

♦ Explanation:

- updatemenus: Adds a **dropdown menu** for dynamically **filtering the species**.
- Each button in the dropdown makes a **species visible** or **invisible**, giving the user control over what data is shown.

4.3.3 Hover Customization

Plotly allows you to customize the information displayed when you hover over any data point in the plot. This is especially useful for providing additional context or values.

```
python
```

```
# Customize hover information
fig.update_traces(
    hovertemplate='<b>Species:
%{text}</b><br>Sepal    Width:    %{x}<br>Sepal
Length: %{y}<extra></extra>',
    text=df['species']
)
```

```
# Show the plot
fig.show()
```

⬧ Explanation:

- `hovertemplate`: Customizes the content shown when hovering over data points.
- `text=df['species']`: Displays the species name when hovering over each point.

4.4 Summary and Next Steps

In this chapter, we explored:

- **Plotly's capabilities** for creating **interactive charts**, including **scatter plots**, **bar plots**, and **line plots**.
- How to **customize** Plotly charts with **layout adjustments**, **interactive widgets**, and **hover features**.

Next Chapter: Creating Dashboards with Dash

In the next chapter, we'll take a deeper dive into **Dash**, a framework built on top of Plotly, to create **interactive web-based dashboards** that showcase data in real-time and provide advanced functionality for user interaction.

◆ **Key Takeaway**: Plotly transforms static visualizations into **interactive, web-based tools** that enable dynamic data exploration and in-depth analysis. 🚀

CHAPTER 5

Understanding Dashboard Creation

5.1 Introduction to Dashboards and Their Purpose

A **dashboard** is a **visual representation** of key metrics, data points, or performance indicators. Dashboards are designed to provide at-a-glance views of **important business or operational data**, allowing users to **track progress**, **identify trends**, and **make informed decisions** quickly.

Dashboards are used in various industries, such as **business intelligence**, **finance**, **healthcare**, and **marketing**, to monitor metrics like sales performance, customer engagement, or website traffic in real-time. They serve as **centralized hubs** for visualizing and interpreting data, streamlining decision-making processes, and improving productivity.

Why Dashboards Are Important

- **Real-Time Insights**: Dashboards provide **real-time data visualization**, helping users make timely, data-driven decisions.

- **Centralized Information**: By aggregating important data in one place, dashboards eliminate the need to search through multiple reports or data sources.
- **Data-Driven Decisions**: Dashboards present data in a visually compelling way, which helps decision-makers understand complex information quickly and make informed choices.
- **Actionable Metrics**: Dashboards are designed to highlight **critical metrics** and **KPIs** (Key Performance Indicators), allowing users to focus on what's most important.

Types of Dashboards

- **Operational Dashboards**: Monitor day-to-day operations and real-time metrics.
- **Analytical Dashboards**: Provide in-depth analysis of data, helping with **trend analysis, predictive analytics**, and **performance reviews**.
- **Strategic Dashboards**: Display long-term trends and **big-picture insights** for executives and senior management to track overall business performance.

5.2 Key Elements of a Successful Dashboard

Creating a successful dashboard involves more than just displaying a bunch of charts and graphs. The goal is to **present data in a meaningful way** that helps users quickly absorb key information and make decisions.

5.2.1 Clear Purpose and Audience

Before you start creating a dashboard, it's essential to define its **purpose** and understand its **audience**. A dashboard designed for an executive team may be different from one created for a data analyst. Define the key **metrics** and **KPIs** that are most relevant to the users.

5.2.2 Simplicity and Clarity

Dashboards should prioritize **clarity** and **simplicity**. The visual elements should not overwhelm the user with too much information. **Focus on key metrics** and provide easy-to-read visuals that allow for **quick interpretation**.

- **Use of space**: Ensure there is enough whitespace between elements, so the dashboard doesn't appear cluttered.
- **Avoid information overload**: Keep the number of visual elements manageable to ensure users aren't distracted by unnecessary details.

5.2.3 Interactivity

Dashboards should allow users to interact with the data. **Interactive elements** like dropdown menus, sliders, and buttons help users customize the view according to their needs. Interactivity allows for deeper data exploration without the need to create multiple static reports.

5.2.4 Visual Hierarchy

Establish a **visual hierarchy** where the most important data points are placed **prominently**. This helps users focus on what matters most, allowing them to quickly get a sense of the **current state** of the business or operation.

- **Positioning**: Place **critical metrics** at the top or in the most prominent areas of the dashboard.
- **Colors and Size**: Use color and size to emphasize key data points. For example, use **red** to indicate negative trends and **green** to highlight positive metrics.

5.2.5 Consistent Design

A consistent design ensures that users can **easily navigate** and **interpret** the dashboard. Maintain uniformity in **colors**, **fonts**, and **icons** to create a visually cohesive experience.

- **Color Palette**: Use a limited and consistent color palette to avoid overwhelming users.
- **Fonts**: Stick to a small number of fonts for **clarity** and **legibility**.

5.2.6 Performance

Dashboards should be **fast** and responsive, even when dealing with **large datasets**. Slow-loading dashboards can frustrate users and lead to poor adoption. Optimize for performance by using efficient data queries and minimizing the number of elements on the dashboard.

5.3 Introduction to Dash for Creating Web-Based Dashboards

Now that you understand the purpose and key elements of a successful dashboard, let's dive into **Dash**, a Python framework for creating **interactive, web-based dashboards**. Dash is built on top of **Plotly** and integrates well with **Pandas** to create dynamic and interactive web applications.

Dash allows you to create dashboards with **Python code** rather than relying on JavaScript or front-end web development, making it an ideal tool for Python developers. With Dash, you can create dashboards that allow users to interact with data, filter results, and visualize complex datasets.

5.3.1 Installing Dash

To get started with Dash, you first need to install it along with **Plotly** for visualization:

```bash
```

```
pip install dash plotly
```

Once installed, you can import Dash and start building your first interactive dashboard.

5.3.2 Basic Structure of a Dash App

A Dash app typically consists of:

- **Layout**: Defines the structure of the dashboard, including graphs, text, and interactive components.

- **Callbacks**: Define interactivity, specifying how input elements (like sliders or dropdowns) control the content of the dashboard.

Here's a simple Dash app example that creates a basic **scatter plot**:

python

```python
import dash
from dash import dcc, html
import plotly.express as px

# Initialize the Dash app
app = dash.Dash(__name__)

# Load the dataset
df = px.data.iris()

# Define the layout of the app
app.layout = html.Div([
    html.H1("Interactive  Scatter  Plot:  Iris
Dataset"),
    dcc.Graph(
        id='scatter-plot',
        figure=px.scatter(df,  x='sepal_width',
y='sepal_length', color='species')
    )
])
```

```
# Run the app
if __name__ == '__main__':
    app.run_server(debug=True)
```

◆ Explanation:

- `html.Div()`: Defines a **container** for the content of the dashboard.
- `dcc.Graph()`: Embeds a **Plotly graph** in the layout.
- `px.scatter()`: Creates an **interactive scatter plot** using Plotly.

5.3.3 Adding Interactivity to Dashboards

One of the key strengths of Dash is the ability to add **interactive elements** to your dashboards, such as **dropdowns, sliders,** and **buttons**. Let's create a more advanced app where the user can select the species from a dropdown and update the scatter plot accordingly:

python

```
from dash import dcc, html
import dash
import plotly.express as px
from dash.dependencies import Input, Output
```

```python
# Initialize the Dash app
app = dash.Dash(__name__)

# Load the dataset
df = px.data.iris()

# Define the layout with a dropdown and scatter
plot
app.layout = html.Div([
    html.H1("Interactive    Scatter    Plot:    Iris
Dataset"),
    dcc.Dropdown(
        id='species-dropdown',
        options=[
            {'label': species, 'value': species}
for species in df['species'].unique()
        ],
        value='setosa'  # Default value
    ),
    dcc.Graph(id='scatter-plot')
])

# Define the callback to update the scatter plot
@app.callback(
    Output('scatter-plot', 'figure'),
    [Input('species-dropdown', 'value')]
)
def update_plot(selected_species):
```

```
    filtered_df      =      df[df['species']      ==
selected_species]
    return                 px.scatter(filtered_df,
x='sepal_width',                  y='sepal_length',
color='species')


# Run the app
if __name__ == '__main__':
    app.run_server(debug=True)
```

✦ **Explanation**:

- `dcc.Dropdown()`: Adds a dropdown menu to select the species.
- The **callback** function updates the scatter plot based on the selected species.

5.4 Summary and Next Steps

In this chapter, we covered:

- **The purpose of dashboards**: Dashboards help visualize key metrics and enable data-driven decision-making.
- **Key elements of successful dashboards**: Simplicity, clarity, interactivity, and performance.

- **Introduction to Dash**: We explored how to create **interactive, web-based dashboards** using Dash, integrating **Plotly charts** and **user inputs** for real-time data exploration.

Next Chapter: Advanced Dash Features and Real-Time Dashboards

In the next chapter, we will explore advanced Dash features, including **callbacks**, **dynamic updates**, and **real-time data streaming** to create more sophisticated, interactive dashboards.

◆ **Key Takeaway**: Dash is a powerful tool for creating **interactive web dashboards** that allow users to interact with data, explore trends, and make informed decisions. 🚀

PART 2

ESSENTIAL VISUALIZATION TECHNIQUES

CHAPTER 6:

Visualizing Time-Series Data

6.1 Best Practices for Visualizing Time-Series Data

Time-series data refers to data points collected or recorded at **specific time intervals**, often used to track trends, cycles, and patterns over time. The goal when visualizing time-series data is to present trends, changes, and fluctuations clearly, helping decision-makers spot important patterns or anomalies.

Here are some **best practices** for visualizing time-series data effectively:

1. Use Clear Time Units

Ensure that the **time scale** (e.g., hours, days, weeks, months) is clearly labeled and consistent across your visualization. This allows viewers to interpret the data correctly.

2. Focus on Key Trends

The primary purpose of visualizing time-series data is to highlight **patterns**, **trends**, and **changes** over time. Avoid

75

cluttering the graph with unnecessary data points. Focus on the critical time periods and the most significant trends.

3. Avoid Over-Plotting

Over-plotting, or displaying too many data points on a single plot, can make time-series data difficult to read. **Aggregate data** where appropriate (e.g., by day, week, or month) to reduce the complexity.

4. Choose the Right Plot Type

Different types of time-series visualizations work best for different purposes:

- **Line plots** are great for showing trends over time.
- **Area plots** can show cumulative data.
- **Bar plots** can be used when there are distinct time intervals or categories.

5. Highlight Key Events

If there are significant events that affect the time-series (e.g., product launches, market crashes), it's helpful to highlight these on the graph with **annotations** or **vertical lines**.

6.2 Creating Line Plots and Area Plots

6.2.1 Line Plots

A **line plot** is one of the most common ways to visualize time-series data. It is ideal for showing **continuous trends** over time.

Here's how to create a simple line plot with **Plotly**:

python

```
import plotly.express as px

# Load the example data (you can use any time-
series data here)
df = px.data.stocks()

# Create a line plot
fig = px.line(df, x='date', y='GOOG',
title='Google Stock Prices Over Time')

# Show the plot
fig.show()
```

◆ **Explanation**:

- `px.line()`: Creates a **line plot** for time-series data.

77

- `x='date'`: Sets the **time variable** on the x-axis.
- `y='GOOG'`: Specifies the **stock symbol** (Google stock in this case) on the y-axis.

6.2.2 Area Plots

Area plots are similar to line plots but with the area below the line filled in. This visualization helps emphasize the magnitude of the values over time, making it easy to see how the value changes over a period.

python

```
# Create an area plot
fig = px.area(df, x='date', y='GOOG',
title='Google Stock Prices Over Time (Area
Plot)')

# Show the plot
fig.show()
```

◆ **Explanation**:

- `px.area()`: Creates an **area plot**, which fills the space under the line.

Area plots are particularly useful when you want to show the **total value** over time or compare multiple categories over the same period.

6.3 Using Rolling Averages for Trend Visualization

6.3.1 What Are Rolling Averages?

A **rolling average** (or moving average) smooths out fluctuations in time-series data, making it easier to spot **trends** and **patterns**. By averaging data over a specific time window (e.g., 7 days, 30 days), rolling averages eliminate short-term fluctuations.

There are several types of rolling averages:

- **Simple Moving Average (SMA)**: The average of the last n data points.
- **Exponential Moving Average (EMA)**: Gives more weight to recent data points, making it more sensitive to recent trends.

6.3.2 Creating a Rolling Average in Python

Let's use a **7-day rolling average** to smooth Google stock prices over time.

```python
import pandas as pd

# Load the data and calculate the rolling average
df['GOOG_7_day_avg']                              =
df['GOOG'].rolling(window=7).mean()

# Create a line plot with the rolling average
fig   =   px.line(df,   x='date',   y=['GOOG',
'GOOG_7_day_avg'],
                title='Google Stock Prices with 7-
Day Rolling Average')

# Show the plot
fig.show()
```

◆ **Explanation**:

- `rolling(window=7).mean()`: Calculates the **7-day rolling average** for the GOOG column.
- `y=['GOOG', 'GOOG_7_day_avg']`: Plots both the **original data** and the **smoothed trend**.

6.3.3 Why Use Rolling Averages?

Rolling averages help:

- **Smooth out volatility**: By averaging data over a period, you can reduce the noise and focus on the underlying trend.
- **Identify long-term trends**: Rolling averages are especially useful for identifying **long-term changes** and trends in data that may be hidden by short-term fluctuations.

6.4 Advanced Trend Visualization

6.4.1 Adding Annotations for Key Events

To make time-series visualizations more informative, you can add **annotations** to highlight key events or changes in the data.

python

```
# Create a line plot with an annotation
fig = px.line(df, x='date', y='GOOG',
title='Google Stock Prices with Key Event')
```

```
# Add an annotation for a key event (e.g., product
launch)
fig.add_annotation(
    x='2019-06-01', y=1500,
    text='Product Launch',
    showarrow=True,
    arrowhead=2
)

# Show the plot
fig.show()
```

◆ **Explanation**:

- `add_annotation()`: Adds a custom **annotation** at a specific point in the time-series.
- `x='2019-06-01'`: Specifies the date where the event occurred.
- `showarrow=True`: Displays an **arrow** pointing to the annotation.

6.5 Summary and Next Steps

In this chapter, we learned how to effectively visualize **time-series data** using Plotly. We covered:

- Best practices for visualizing time-series data, including choosing the right plot and focusing on trends.
- How to create **line plots** and **area plots** to visualize trends over time.
- The power of **rolling averages** for **smoothing data** and identifying long-term patterns.
- How to add **annotations** to highlight key events or changes in your time-series data.

Next Chapter: Visualizing Categorical Data

In the next chapter, we will explore how to visualize **categorical data**, using **bar charts**, **pie charts**, and more advanced categorical plots in **Seaborn**.

◆ **Key Takeaway**: Time-series visualization is essential for understanding trends and patterns in data. **Rolling averages** and interactive visualizations can help you uncover insights and make better, data-driven decisions. 🚀

CHAPTER 7

Creating Categorical Plots

7.1 Understanding Bar Charts, Pie Charts, and Stacked Bar Charts

Categorical data represents information that can be divided into groups or categories, such as **gender**, **product type**, or **region**. Visualizing categorical data is essential to understanding the **distribution**, **comparisons**, and **relationships** between different categories. In this section, we'll explore the most common categorical plots, including **bar charts**, **pie charts**, and **stacked bar charts**.

7.1.1 Bar Charts

A **bar chart** is used to show the frequency or count of items in a categorical variable. The length of each bar represents the size of the category, making it easy to compare the size of different categories.

python

```
import plotly.express as px
```

```
# Load an example dataset
df = px.data.tips()

# Create a bar chart of total bill by day
fig  =  px.bar(df,  x='day',  y='total_bill',
color='sex',
            title='Bar Chart: Total Bill by Day
and Gender')

# Show the plot
fig.show()
```

✦ Explanation:

- `px.bar()`: Creates a **bar chart** with `day` on the x-axis and `total_bill` on the y-axis.
- `color='sex'`: Colors the bars based on **gender**.
- The **interactive features** of Plotly (e.g., hover, zoom) allow deeper exploration of the data.

7.1.2 Pie Charts

A **pie chart** is a circular chart divided into slices to illustrate numerical proportions. Each slice represents a category's contribution to the whole.

```
python
```

85

```
# Create a pie chart of tips by gender
fig        =        px.pie(df,        names='sex',
values='total_bill',  title='Pie   Chart:   Total
Bill by Gender')

# Show the plot
fig.show()
```

◆ Explanation:

- `px.pie()`: Creates a **pie chart**, where the `names` parameter specifies the categories (gender) and `values` represent the size of each category (total bill).
- **Pie charts** are useful for showing **percentage breakdowns** of categorical data.

7.1.3 Stacked Bar Charts

A **stacked bar chart** shows the **total value** of a categorical variable with segments representing sub-categories. This type of chart is useful for comparing the total size of each category and the relative proportions of sub-categories within each.

```
python
```

86

```
# Create a stacked bar chart of total bill by day
and gender
fig = px.bar(df, x='day', y='total_bill',
color='sex',
            title='Stacked Bar Chart: Total
Bill by Day and Gender',
            text_auto=True)

# Show the plot
fig.show()
```

◆ Explanation:

- `color='sex'`: Stacks the bars by **gender**.
- `text_auto=True`: Adds the total bill values directly on top of each bar segment for clarity.

7.2 Visualizing Categorical Variables: Seaborn's Categorical Plots

Seaborn provides a high-level interface for creating **categorical plots,** making it easier to visualize relationships between categorical and numerical variables. Some of the most commonly used Seaborn categorical plots include **box plots, violin plots, count plots,** and **strip plots**.

7.2.1 Box Plots

A **box plot** displays the distribution of data based on five summary statistics: the minimum, first quartile (Q1), median (Q2), third quartile (Q3), and maximum. It also highlights potential **outliers** in the data.

python

```python
import seaborn as sns
import matplotlib.pyplot as plt

# Create a box plot for total bill by day
sns.boxplot(x='day',  y='total_bill',  data=df,
palette='coolwarm')

# Add title and labels
plt.title('Box Plot: Total Bill by Day')
plt.xlabel('Day of the Week')
plt.ylabel('Total Bill ($)')

# Show the plot
plt.show()
```

◆ **Explanation**:

- `sns.boxplot()`: Creates a **box plot** of `total_bill` grouped by `day`.

88

- Box plots are great for visualizing **distributions**, **medians**, and identifying **outliers**.

7.2.2 Violin Plots

A **violin plot** combines aspects of a **box plot** and a **kernel density plot**. It shows the distribution of the data, highlighting its **density** and **spread**.

```python
# Create a violin plot of total bill by day
sns.violinplot(x='day', y='total_bill', data=df,
palette='muted')

# Add title and labels
plt.title('Violin Plot: Total Bill by Day')
plt.xlabel('Day of the Week')
plt.ylabel('Total Bill ($)')

# Show the plot
plt.show()
```

◆ Explanation:

- `sns.violinplot()`: Creates a **violin plot** that shows both the distribution and the density of `total_bill` by day.

- Violin plots provide **a deeper understanding** of the **distribution** compared to box plots.

7.2.3 Count Plots

A **count plot** is a bar plot that shows the count of occurrences of each category.

python

```
# Create a count plot for days of the week
sns.countplot(x='day', data=df, palette='Set1')

# Add title and labels
plt.title('Count Plot: Count of Days')
plt.xlabel('Day of the Week')
plt.ylabel('Count')

# Show the plot
plt.show()
```

◆ **Explanation**:

- `sns.countplot()`: Creates a **count plot** for the variable `day`, showing how many times each day appears in the dataset.
- Count plots are particularly useful for visualizing the **frequency distribution** of categorical data.

7.2.4 Strip Plots

A **strip plot** is a scatter plot for categorical data. It places data points along a categorical axis, showing individual observations.

```python
# Create a strip plot of total bill by day
sns.stripplot(x='day', y='total_bill', data=df,
jitter=True, color='black')

# Add title and labels
plt.title('Strip Plot: Total Bill by Day')
plt.xlabel('Day of the Week')
plt.ylabel('Total Bill ($)')

# Show the plot
plt.show()
```

⬥ **Explanation**:

- `sns.stripplot()`: Creates a **strip plot**, which places individual `total_bill` data points along the `day` categories.
- `jitter=True`: Adds a small random horizontal displacement to make overlapping points more visible.

91

7.3 Advanced Categorical Visualizations with Plotly

Plotly allows for more **dynamic and interactive categorical visualizations**, enhancing the user experience with **hovering**, **filtering**, and **zooming** capabilities.

7.3.1 Customizing Bar Plots with Plotly

You can create customized and interactive bar charts using Plotly's **Bar charts** to visualize categorical data in a more dynamic way.

python

```
import plotly.graph_objects as go

# Create a bar chart for total bill by day
fig   =   go.Figure(data=[go.Bar(x=df['day'],
y=df['total_bill'], marker_color='green')])

# Customize layout and add title
fig.update_layout(title='Bar  Chart:  Total  Bill
by Day',
                  xaxis_title='Day of the Week',
                  yaxis_title='Total Bill ($)')
```

```
# Show the plot
fig.show()
```

◆ Explanation:

- go.Figure(): Creates a **Plotly figure** that contains a **bar chart**.
- update_layout(): Customizes the chart layout and labels.

7.3.2 Interactive Pie Charts

Plotly allows you to create interactive pie charts with additional features like **hover information** and **click events**.

```
python
```

```
# Create an interactive pie chart for tips by
gender
fig        =        px.pie(df,        names='sex',
values='total_bill',    title='Pie    Chart:    Total
Bill by Gender')

# Show the plot
fig.show()
```

◆ Explanation:

- `px.pie()`: Creates an **interactive pie chart** that shows the distribution of `total_bill` by `sex`.
- **Hover**: Hovering over each slice provides more details about the category and its contribution.

7.4 Summary and Next Steps

In this chapter, we:

- Explored the most common **categorical plots**, including **bar charts**, **pie charts**, and **stacked bar charts**, for visualizing the distribution and comparisons of categories.
- Learned how to use **Seaborn** to create **box plots**, **violin plots**, **count plots**, and **strip plots** to visualize categorical variables effectively.
- Delved into **Plotly** for creating **interactive** and **dynamic** visualizations, including **customized bar charts** and **interactive pie charts**.

Next Chapter: Heatmaps and Correlation Plots

In the next chapter, we will explore how to visualize **relationships between variables** using **heatmaps** and

correlation matrices, and how to interpret these visualizations to uncover deeper insights from your data.

◆ **Key Takeaway**: Categorical plots, whether static or interactive, provide powerful insights into the distribution and relationships of categories in your dataset, helping you make informed, data-driven decisions. 🚀

CHAPTER 8

Heatmaps and Correlation Matrices

8.1 Visualizing Correlations with Heatmaps

A **heatmap** is a powerful data visualization tool that displays data in a matrix format, with values represented by varying colors. It's especially useful for visualizing the **relationships between variables** and **identifying correlations** in your dataset. **Correlation heatmaps** are a popular application of heatmaps, as they allow you to easily observe how different variables relate to one another.

What is Correlation?

- **Correlation** refers to the relationship between two variables. If the correlation is positive, as one variable increases, the other also increases. If it's negative, as one increases, the other decreases.
- A **correlation matrix** is a table showing correlation coefficients between variables, where each cell in the matrix represents the correlation between two variables.

A **heatmap** visualizes this matrix, with colors representing the strength of correlations:

- **Dark colors** typically represent **strong correlations** (either positive or negative).
- **Light colors** indicate **weak correlations**.

8.1.1 Creating a Basic Heatmap with Plotly

Plotly allows you to create interactive heatmaps, which can be especially useful for exploring relationships in large datasets.

python

```
import plotly.express as px
import pandas as pd

# Load example dataset
df = px.data.tips()

# Compute the correlation matrix
corr_matrix = df.corr()

# Create a heatmap
fig = px.imshow(corr_matrix, text_auto=True,
color_continuous_scale='Blues',
             title="Correlation Heatmap")

# Show the plot
fig.show()
```

◆ **Explanation**:

- `df.corr()`: Calculates the **correlation matrix** for the numerical columns of the DataFrame.
- `px.imshow()`: Creates an interactive **heatmap** where each cell represents the correlation between two variables.
- `text_auto=True`: Automatically adds correlation values inside each cell for clarity.

8.2 Customizing Heatmaps for Readability

When dealing with large datasets, **heatmaps** can become overwhelming if not properly designed. Here are some customization tips to improve **readability** and highlight the important information:

8.2.1 Adjusting Color Scales

The color scale is one of the most important elements of a heatmap, as it communicates the strength of the correlations. You can use different **color palettes** and **scales** to improve the clarity of the plot.

```python
python
```

```
# Create a heatmap with a custom color scale
fig  =  px.imshow(corr_matrix,  text_auto=True,
color_continuous_scale='RdBu_r',
                title="Customized    Correlation
Heatmap")

# Show the plot
fig.show()
```

♦ **Explanation**:

- `color_continuous_scale='RdBu_r'`: The **'Red-Blue reversed'** color scale is commonly used to indicate positive and negative correlations, with **red** representing strong positive correlation and **blue** representing negative correlation.
- **Custom color scales** can make correlations stand out more clearly, especially when dealing with both positive and negative values.

8.2.2 Adding Annotations

Annotations allow you to display **numeric values** in the cells of the heatmap. This can help to better communicate the strength of correlations and add clarity.

```
python
```

```
# Create a heatmap with annotations
fig  =  px.imshow(corr_matrix,  text_auto=True,
color_continuous_scale='Viridis',
                  title="Correlation  Heatmap  with
Annotations")

# Show the plot
fig.show()
```

◆ **Explanation**:

- `text_auto=True`: Automatically adds the correlation **values** inside the cells of the heatmap for easier interpretation.

8.2.3 Clustering Variables

In larger datasets, grouping similar variables together in the heatmap can make it easier to understand relationships. This can be done using **hierarchical clustering** to reorder the rows and columns based on similarity.

python

```
import seaborn as sns
import matplotlib.pyplot as plt

# Create a heatmap with hierarchical clustering
```

```
sns.clustermap(corr_matrix,        annot=True,
cmap='coolwarm', figsize=(10, 8))

# Show the plot
plt.show()
```

✦ Explanation:

- `sns.clustermap()`: Automatically applies **hierarchical clustering** to reorder the heatmap's rows and columns, grouping similar variables together.
- `annot=True`: Displays the correlation values within the heatmap.

8.3 Plotting Correlation Matrices with Seaborn

Seaborn is another excellent tool for creating heatmaps and correlation matrices. It provides functions like `heatmap()` and `clustermap()` that are ideal for visualizing correlations.

8.3.1 Creating a Basic Heatmap with Seaborn

Let's create a correlation heatmap using **Seaborn**, which is particularly well-suited for handling **Pandas DataFrames** and producing aesthetically pleasing plots.

```python
python

import seaborn as sns
import matplotlib.pyplot as plt

# Load the dataset
df = sns.load_dataset('tips')

# Calculate the correlation matrix
corr_matrix = df.corr()

# Create a Seaborn heatmap
plt.figure(figsize=(10, 8))
sns.heatmap(corr_matrix,              annot=True,
cmap='coolwarm', linewidths=0.5, fmt='.2f')

# Add title
plt.title('Correlation Matrix Heatmap')

# Show the plot
plt.show()
```

◆ Explanation:

- `sns.heatmap()`: Creates the **heatmap** visualization using Seaborn.
- `annot=True`: Adds the correlation **values** in each cell.

- `cmap='coolwarm'`: Chooses the **'coolwarm'** color palette, where blue represents negative correlations and red represents positive correlations.

- `linewidths=0.5`: Adds a small border between the cells to improve readability.

- `fmt='.2f'`: Formats the correlation values to two decimal places.

8.3.2 Using a Clustermap for Better Grouping

Seaborn's **clustermap** function provides the ability to **cluster** rows and columns in the correlation matrix, making it easier to spot patterns in the data.

python

```
# Create a clustermap with Seaborn
sns.clustermap(corr_matrix,        annot=True,
cmap='YlGnBu', figsize=(10, 8))

# Show the plot
plt.show()
```

✦ **Explanation**:

- `sns.clustermap()`: This function not only visualizes the heatmap but also applies **hierarchical clustering** to reorder rows and columns.

103

- `cmap='YlGnBu'`: Uses the **'Yellow-Green-Blue'** color palette.

8.4 Summary and Next Steps

In this chapter, we explored:

- **Heatmaps** as a tool for visualizing correlations, identifying patterns, and relationships between variables.
- How to **customize** heatmaps with different **color scales**, **annotations**, and **clustering** to improve readability and interpretation.
- Creating correlation matrices with **Seaborn** and **Plotly**, and how to visualize and analyze complex data relationships.

Next Chapter: Visualizing Relationships Between Multiple Variables

In the next chapter, we will explore techniques for visualizing **relationships** between multiple variables, using **pair plots**, **scatter matrix plots**, and more advanced visualizations in Seaborn and Plotly.

◆ **Key Takeaway**: Heatmaps and correlation matrices are essential tools for understanding **relationships between variables**. With proper customization, you can turn a simple matrix into a powerful and actionable visualization that reveals valuable insights in your data. 🚀

CHAPTER 9

Geographical Data Visualization

9.1 Introduction to Geospatial Data Visualization

Geospatial data visualization is the process of displaying **location-based data** on a map or geographical surface to uncover patterns, trends, and relationships that are tied to specific locations. This type of visualization is extremely useful for businesses, urban planners, environmental scientists, and anyone who needs to analyze data with a **spatial** or **geographical component**.

For example, you might want to visualize **sales performance** across different regions, **climate data** across countries, or **population density** in cities. By plotting this data on a **map**, it becomes easier to see trends and identify geographical patterns that could be crucial for decision-making.

Why Geospatial Visualization Matters

- **Improved Decision-Making**: Geospatial visualizations allow businesses to **make data-driven decisions** by understanding **regional trends** and **patterns**.

- **Location-Based Analysis**: Helps businesses, organizations, or governments understand spatial **inequality, resource distribution**, and **regional performance**.

- **Enhanced Storytelling**: Visualizing data on a map brings context and helps **tell a story** that might be difficult to interpret using traditional charts and graphs.

9.2 Plotting Data on Maps Using Plotly

Plotly makes it easy to create interactive geographical visualizations, allowing users to engage with data on a map and explore regions of interest.

9.2.1 Plotting Simple Maps

One of the easiest ways to visualize data on a map is by plotting **coordinates** (latitude and longitude) to create **scatter plots** on a map. Plotly provides a **scatter mapbox** for this purpose.

```python
python

import plotly.express as px

# Load sample dataset with geographical
coordinates
df = px.data.gapminder()

# Create a scatter map for GDP vs life expectancy
by country
fig = px.scatter_geo(df, locations="iso_alpha",
size="pop", color="continent",
                    hover_name="country",
size_max=100, title="Global Data (GDP vs Life
Expectancy)")

# Show the plot
fig.show()
```

◆ **Explanation**:

- `px.scatter_geo()`: Creates a scatter plot on a **geographical map**.
- `locations="iso_alpha"`: Specifies the ISO country codes.
- `size="pop"`: Represents **population size** through circle size.

- `color="continent"`: Colors the markers based on the continent.

This creates an interactive map where you can hover over each country to get more information and zoom in on different areas.

9.2.2 Customizing Map Styles

Plotly offers various customization options for map styles. You can change the map style to suit your visual preferences.

```python
python
```

```python
fig.update_geos(projection_type="natural earth",
showcoastlines=True, coastlinecolor="black")

fig.show()
```

⬥ **Explanation**:

- `update_geos()`: Customizes the geographical features of the map.
- `projection_type="natural earth"`: Uses the **Natural Earth projection** for a more aesthetically pleasing map style.
- `showcoastlines=True`: Displays the **coastlines** of countries.

9.3 Creating Choropleth Maps and Scatter Maps

9.3.1 Choropleth Maps

Choropleth maps use **color shading** to represent the values of a variable over geographic regions. These maps are ideal for visualizing data such as **population density**, **GDP**, or **crime rates** by country, state, or region. The color intensity indicates the magnitude of the data in each region.

python

```
# Create a choropleth map for GDP by country
fig = px.choropleth(df, locations="iso_alpha",
color="gdpPercap", hover_name="country",

color_continuous_scale="Viridis", title="GDP per
Capita by Country")

# Show the plot
fig.show()
```

◆ Explanation:

- `px.choropleth()`: Creates a **choropleth map**, where `color` is based on the `gdpPercap` column (GDP per capita).
- `color_continuous_scale="Viridis"`: Uses the **Viridis** color scale for better visibility of data values.
- `hover_name="country"`: Shows the country name when hovering over the regions.

9.3.2 Customizing Choropleth Maps

You can fine-tune the appearance and functionality of choropleth maps by adjusting **color scales**, adding **hover information**, and customizing map regions.

python

```
# Customize the choropleth map with hover
information and a new color scale
fig.update_geos(showland=True,
landcolor="lightgray")

fig.update_traces(marker_line_width=0.5,
marker_line_color="white")

fig.show()
```

◆ **Explanation**:

111

- `update_geos()`: Enables the display of land areas with customized colors (`lightgray`).
- `update_traces()`: Changes the line width and color for region borders to make the map more readable.

9.3.3 Scatter Maps

Scatter maps plot **individual data points** on a geographical map based on their **longitude and latitude**. These maps are great for visualizing the distribution of points, such as **customer locations**, **sales representatives**, or **event data**.

python

```python
# Example dataset of city locations
df_cities = pd.DataFrame({
    "City": ["New York", "London", "Tokyo",
"Paris", "Berlin"],
    "Latitude": [40.7128, 51.5074, 35.6762,
48.8566, 52.52],
    "Longitude": [-74.0060, -0.1278, 139.6503,
2.3522, 13.4050]
})

# Plot scatter map
fig = px.scatter_geo(df_cities, lat="Latitude",
lon="Longitude", text="City",
```

```
                      title="City Locations")

# Show the plot
fig.show()
```

◆ **Explanation**:

- `px.scatter_geo()`: Plots **individual data points** based on **latitude** and **longitude**.
- `text="City"`: Labels each point with the corresponding city name.

Scatter maps allow for precise visualization of **location data** and can be enhanced with interactive features, such as **zooming** and **hovering**.

9.4 Summary and Next Steps

In this chapter, we explored **geospatial data visualization**, focusing on:

- The importance of visualizing **location-based data** to uncover spatial trends and patterns.
- How to plot geographical data using **Plotly** to create **scatter maps** and **choropleth maps**.

- How to customize maps by adjusting map styles, adding hover features, and fine-tuning color scales.

Next Chapter: Advanced Geospatial Visualization

In the next chapter, we will dive deeper into **advanced geospatial visualizations**, such as **3D maps, geojson data visualization**, and **interactive maps** with real-time data updates.

◆ **Key Takeaway**: Geospatial visualizations allow you to transform location-based data into interactive, insightful visualizations that reveal critical patterns tied to specific regions. With **Plotly**, you can create stunning and highly interactive maps that help make better, data-driven decisions. 🚀

CHAPTER 10

Creating Histograms and Distribution Plots

10.1 Visualizing the Distribution of Data

Histograms and **distribution plots** are essential tools for understanding the distribution of a dataset. These visualizations help you identify key characteristics of the data, such as its **central tendency**, **spread**, **shape**, and **outliers**. When dealing with continuous data, these plots provide a clear way to see how data points are distributed across different ranges.

Why Visualize Data Distribution?

- **Central Tendency**: Distribution plots reveal where the center of the data lies, often represented by the **mean** or **median**.
- **Spread**: They show the **range** and **variability** of the data, including how spread out the values are.
- **Shape**: They help identify the **shape** of the distribution, such as whether it is **normal**, **skewed**, or **bimodal**.

115

- **Outliers**: Distribution plots highlight **outliers** and extreme values that may require further attention.

10.2 Creating Histograms

A **histogram** is a bar graph that shows the frequency of data points falling within specified **bins**. Each bar represents the count (or proportion) of values within a particular range. It's an excellent tool for **visualizing the distribution** of a dataset.

10.2.1 Basic Histogram

Here's how to create a simple histogram using **Plotly** to visualize the distribution of a dataset:

```python
python


import plotly.express as px

# Load a sample dataset
df = px.data.tips()

# Create a histogram of the total bill amounts
fig = px.histogram(df, x='total_bill', nbins=20,
title="Histogram of Total Bill Amounts")
```

```
# Show the plot
fig.show()
```

◆ **Explanation**:

- `px.histogram()`: Creates a **histogram** where `x='total_bill'` represents the variable to be plotted.
- `nbins=20`: Specifies the number of **bins** in the histogram, which determines how the data is grouped.
- **Histogram** shows how the `total_bill` values are distributed across different ranges.

10.2.2 Customizing Histograms

Histograms can be customized to make them more informative and aesthetically pleasing. Here are some customization options:

```python
fig.update_traces(marker_color='orange',
opacity=0.7,
                marker_line_width=1.5,
marker_line_color='black')
```

```
fig.update_layout(bargap=0.1, xaxis_title="Total
Bill", yaxis_title="Frequency")
```

```
fig.show()
```

◆ **Explanation**:

- `marker_color='orange'`: Sets the color of the bars to **orange**.
- `opacity=0.7`: Adjusts the transparency of the bars.
- `bargap=0.1`: Controls the **gap** between bars to prevent overlap.
- `xaxis_title` and `yaxis_title`: Add **axis labels** for clarity.

10.3 Creating Kernel Density Estimation (KDE) Plots

A **KDE plot** is a smooth, continuous representation of the distribution of data. Unlike a histogram, which uses discrete bins, a **KDE plot** shows a **smooth curve** that helps you better understand the underlying distribution, especially for large datasets.

10.3.1 Creating a KDE Plot

You can create a **KDE plot** with **Seaborn**, which is well-suited for visualizing distributions with smooth curves:

python

```python
import seaborn as sns
import matplotlib.pyplot as plt

# Create a KDE plot for the total bill amounts
sns.kdeplot(df['total_bill'],          shade=True,
color='blue')

# Add title and labels
plt.title("KDE Plot of Total Bill Amounts")
plt.xlabel("Total Bill ($)")
plt.ylabel("Density")

# Show the plot
plt.show()
```

✦ **Explanation**:

- `sns.kdeplot()`: Creates a **Kernel Density Estimate** plot for the `total_bill` column.
- `shade=True`: Fills the area under the curve for better visibility.

119

- The **smooth curve** helps visualize the **density** of the data, showing where most values are concentrated.

10.3.2 Customizing KDE Plots

You can adjust several parameters to fine-tune your KDE plot, such as the **bandwidth, colors**, and **linestyle**.

python

```
sns.kdeplot(df['total_bill'],           shade=True,
color='purple', linewidth=3, bw_adjust=0.5)

plt.title("Customized KDE Plot of Total Bill
Amounts")
plt.xlabel("Total Bill ($)")
plt.ylabel("Density")

plt.show()
```

◆ **Explanation**:

- `linewidth=3`: Adjusts the width of the **KDE line**.
- `bw_adjust=0.5`: Controls the **bandwidth** of the KDE, affecting the smoothness of the curve.

10.4 Creating Rug Plots

A **rug plot** is a simple way to show individual data points along the x-axis. It's often combined with a KDE plot to provide a clearer picture of the distribution.

10.4.1 Creating a Rug Plot

You can add a **rug plot** to a KDE plot to show individual data points along the x-axis:

python

```
sns.kdeplot(df['total_bill',        shade=True,
color='green', rug=True)

plt.title("KDE Plot with Rug Plot of Total Bill
Amounts")
plt.xlabel("Total Bill ($)")
plt.ylabel("Density")

plt.show()
```

◆ **Explanation**:

- rug=True: Adds individual **data points** along the x-axis as **ticks** (rug marks).

- This combination allows you to see the **distribution** and the **individual data points**.

10.5 Using Distribution Plots to Compare Datasets

When you have multiple datasets or variables, comparing their distributions can reveal important insights. Plotly and Seaborn make it easy to visualize and compare **multiple distributions** on the same plot.

10.5.1 Comparing Multiple Distributions (Seaborn)

To compare the distributions of different datasets, you can overlay multiple **KDE plots** on the same axes:

python

```
# Create KDE plots for multiple columns
sns.kdeplot(df['total_bill'],          shade=True,
label='Total Bill', color='blue')
sns.kdeplot(df['tip'], shade=True, label='Tip',
color='red')

plt.title("Comparison  of  Total  Bill  and  Tip
Distributions")
plt.xlabel("Amount ($)")
```

```
plt.ylabel("Density")
plt.legend()

plt.show()
```

◆ Explanation:

- `sns.kdeplot()`: Overlays **two KDE plots**, one for `total_bill` and one for `tip`, to compare their distributions.
- `label='Total Bill'`: Adds a **legend** to differentiate between the two distributions.

10.5.2 Comparing Multiple Distributions (Plotly)

You can also compare distributions using **Plotly** by creating multiple histograms or KDE plots on the same graph:

```python
fig = px.histogram(df, x='total_bill', nbins=20,
color='sex', opacity=0.5,
                title="Comparison  of  Total
Bill Amounts by Gender")

# Show the plot
fig.show()
```

◆ Explanation:

- `color='sex'`: Colors the histogram bars by gender to compare the **distribution of total bill amounts** across different genders.

10.6 Summary and Next Steps

In this chapter, we explored how to visualize and compare data distributions using:

- **Histograms**: Showing the frequency of data across bins.
- **KDE Plots**: Smooth, continuous representations of the data distribution.
- **Rug Plots**: Visualizing individual data points along the x-axis.
- **Comparing Datasets**: Using distribution plots to compare multiple datasets and uncover patterns.

Next Chapter: Advanced Distribution Visualizations

In the next chapter, we will explore **box plots**, **violin plots**, and **pair plots** for more advanced distribution visualizations and comparisons.

◆ **Key Takeaway**: Distribution plots such as **histograms**, **KDEs**, and **rug plots** are essential for understanding how data behaves. Use these visualizations to uncover key patterns, trends, and outliers in your data. 🚀

PART 3

ADVANCED VISUALIZATION
TECHNIQUES

CHAPTER 11

3D Plots and Visualizing Complex Data

11.1 Introduction to 3D Plotting with Matplotlib and Plotly

As the complexity of your data increases, the need for **3D visualizations** becomes more important. While 2D plots can show data along the x and y axes, **3D plots** allow you to visualize **three variables** simultaneously. This is particularly useful for datasets that have multiple continuous variables, as it enables a more complete understanding of relationships between them.

Both **Matplotlib** and **Plotly** are widely used for creating 3D visualizations in Python. Matplotlib is great for **static 3D plots**, while Plotly excels in creating **interactive, web-based 3D plots**.

Why Use 3D Plots?

- **Better Data Representation**: With an additional axis, 3D plots can display **complex relationships** that can't be captured in 2D visualizations.
- **Enhanced Data Exploration**: Interactivity in tools like **Plotly** allows users to **rotate, zoom, and pan**, exploring the data from various angles to gain deeper insights.
- **Visualization of Multivariate Data**: They help represent **multidimensional datasets**, showing how multiple variables interact with each other.

11.2 Creating 3D Scatter Plots and Surface Plots

11.2.1 3D Scatter Plots with Matplotlib

A **3D scatter plot** is used to visualize the relationship between three continuous variables. Each point in a 3D scatter plot is defined by three coordinates: x, y, and z.

Here's how to create a basic 3D scatter plot using **Matplotlib**:

python

```
import matplotlib.pyplot as plt
```

```
from mpl_toolkits.mplot3d import Axes3D
import numpy as np

# Generate random data for the plot
x = np.random.rand(100)
y = np.random.rand(100)
z = np.random.rand(100)

# Create a figure and 3D axis
fig = plt.figure(figsize=(10, 7))
ax = fig.add_subplot(111, projection='3d')

# Create a scatter plot
ax.scatter(x, y, z, c='r', marker='o')

# Add labels
ax.set_xlabel('X Axis')
ax.set_ylabel('Y Axis')
ax.set_zlabel('Z Axis')

# Set title
ax.set_title('3D Scatter Plot')

# Show the plot
plt.show()
```

◆ **Explanation**:

- `ax.scatter(x, y, z)`: Creates a **3D scatter plot** with the variables x, y, and z.
- `c='r'`: Colors the points red.
- `projection='3d'`: Specifies that the plot should be in 3D.

3D scatter plots are useful for visualizing **clusters** and **relationships** between three variables, especially in machine learning or data analysis tasks.

11.2.2 3D Scatter Plots with Plotly

Plotly allows for **interactive** 3D scatter plots where users can **rotate**, **zoom**, and **pan** to explore data from different perspectives.

python

```
import plotly.express as px
import pandas as pd

# Generate a DataFrame with random data
df = pd.DataFrame({
    'x': np.random.rand(100),
    'y': np.random.rand(100),
    'z': np.random.rand(100)
})
```

- `np.meshgrid()`: Creates a grid of x and y values, which is used to calculate the **z-values** for the surface.
- `ax.plot_surface()`: Creates the **3D surface plot** with a color map (`cmap='viridis'`).

Surface plots are particularly useful for visualizing functions of two variables and exploring **topographic patterns**.

11.3 Customizing 3D Plots for Better Clarity and Presentation

Customizing 3D plots is essential to improve clarity, **presentation**, and **interpretation**. Here are some tips for customizing your plots:

11.3.1 Customizing with Matplotlib

- **Color Maps**: Choose an appropriate color map to make the plot more visually appealing and easier to interpret.
- **Lighting**: Adjust the lighting of the 3D plot to enhance the depth and surface definition.

```python
# Adjusting the surface plot with lighting and
color map
```

```
fig = plt.figure(figsize=(10, 7))
ax = fig.add_subplot(111, projection='3d')
ax.plot_surface(x,    y,    z,    cmap='plasma',
edgecolor='k')

ax.set_title('Customized 3D Surface Plot')
plt.show()
```

✦ Explanation:

- edgecolor='k': Adds **black edges** to the surface for better visibility.
- cmap='plasma': Changes the color map to **plasma**, which is visually distinct and helps highlight data.

11.3.2 Customizing with Plotly

- **Interactive Controls**: Add **sliders, buttons,** or **dropdown menus** to make the plot more dynamic.
- **Axis Labels and Titles**: Make sure the axes and titles are clear and descriptive.

```python
fig.update_layout(
    title="Interactive   3D   Surface   Plot   with
Custom Controls",
    scene=dict(
        xaxis_title="X Axis",
```

```
        yaxis_title="Y Axis",
        zaxis_title="Z Axis"
    ),
    margin=dict(l=0, r=0, b=0, t=40)
)

fig.show()
```

✦ **Explanation**:

- `update_layout()`: Updates the layout of the plot, including titles and axis labels.
- `scene=dict(...)`: Specifies the titles for each axis.
- **Margins**: Reduces the margins for better presentation.

11.4 Summary and Next Steps

In this chapter, we covered:

- How to create **3D scatter plots** and **surface plots** using **Matplotlib** and **Plotly**.
- The key differences between **Matplotlib**'s static 3D plots and **Plotly**'s interactive plots.
- How to **customize** 3D plots to improve their clarity, presentation, and usability.

Next Chapter: Advanced Interactive Visualizations

In the next chapter, we will explore more **advanced interactive visualizations**, such as **animation, real-time data visualization**, and **dashboards** using **Plotly** and **Dash**.

◆ **Key Takeaway**: 3D plotting allows you to **visualize complex data** in three dimensions, offering deeper insights and enhancing data interpretation. **Matplotlib** and **Plotly** make it easy to create interactive, customizable 3D visualizations that reveal hidden patterns in your data. 🚀

CHAPTER 12

Advanced Plot Customization with Matplotlib

12.1 Customizing Plot Appearance: Fonts, Colors, and Markers

Matplotlib offers a wide range of customization options to help you refine the appearance of your plots, making them both visually appealing and easy to interpret. In this section, we'll focus on **customizing fonts**, **colors**, and **markers**—all of which can significantly improve the clarity and aesthetics of your visualizations.

12.1.1 Customizing Fonts

Matplotlib allows you to adjust font properties such as size, style, and family to suit your needs.

```python
import matplotlib.pyplot as plt

# Data
```

```
x = [1, 2, 3, 4, 5]
y = [2, 4, 6, 8, 10]

# Create the plot
plt.plot(x, y)

# Customize font properties
plt.title('Custom Font Example', fontsize=16,
fontfamily='serif', fontweight='bold')
plt.xlabel('X        Axis',        fontsize=14,
fontstyle='italic')
plt.ylabel('Y Axis', fontsize=14)

# Show the plot
plt.show()
```

✦ Explanation:

- `fontsize=16`: Sets the font size for the title.
- `fontfamily='serif'`: Specifies the font family (you can also use `'sans-serif'`, `'monospace'`, etc.).
- `fontweight='bold'`: Makes the title **bold**.
- `fontstyle='italic'`: Sets the x-axis label to **italic**.

12.1.2 Customizing Colors

Matplotlib offers a variety of options for customizing the **colors** of plot elements. You can specify colors using basic names, RGB values, or even **colormaps**.

python

```python
# Create a plot with custom colors
plt.plot(x,    y,    color='green',    marker='o',
markersize=8, label='Green Line')

# Add a red line with a dashed style
plt.plot([1,   2,   3,   4,   5],   [1,   2,   3,   4,   5],
color='red',   linestyle='--',   label='Red   Dashed
Line')

# Add title and labels
plt.title('Color      Customization      Example',
fontsize=16)
plt.xlabel('X Axis', fontsize=12)
plt.ylabel('Y Axis', fontsize=12)

# Add a legend
plt.legend()

# Show the plot
plt.show()
```

◆ Explanation:

- `color='green'`: Sets the color of the line to **green**.
- `marker='o'`: Specifies **circle markers** for the data points.
- `markersize=8`: Adjusts the size of the markers.
- `color='red'` and `linestyle='--'`: Creates a **red dashed line**.
- `plt.legend()`: Adds a **legend** to identify the lines.

12.1.3 Customizing Markers

Markers help to highlight individual data points on your plot. Matplotlib offers a wide variety of markers, including circles, squares, and diamonds.

python

```python
# Create a scatter plot with custom markers
plt.plot(x, y, marker='D', markersize=12,
color='purple', linestyle='None', label='Diamond
Marker')

# Show the plot
plt.show()
```

◆ Explanation:

- `marker='D'`: Uses a **diamond** shape for the markers.
- `markersize=12`: Increases the marker size.
- `linestyle='None'`: Removes the line and only displays the markers.

12.2 Adding Annotations, Labels, and Legends

Matplotlib provides several tools to annotate your plots with additional information, such as text labels, arrows, and legends. These annotations improve plot readability and help to highlight important points.

12.2.1 Adding Annotations

Annotations allow you to highlight specific data points or areas in your plot by adding text or arrows.

python

```
# Create a plot
plt.plot(x, y, marker='o')

# Annotate a point on the plot
plt.annotate('Point    (3,    6)',    xy=(3,    6),
xytext=(4, 8),
```

```
           arrowprops=dict(facecolor='black',
arrowstyle='->'),
           fontsize=12, color='blue')

# Add title and labels
plt.title('Plot with Annotations', fontsize=16)
plt.xlabel('X Axis', fontsize=12)
plt.ylabel('Y Axis', fontsize=12)

# Show the plot
plt.show()
```

◆ Explanation:

- `plt.annotate()`: Adds an annotation at a specific point (3, 6) with an arrow pointing to (4, 8).
- `arrowprops=dict(facecolor='black', arrowstyle='->')`: Customizes the **arrow** style and color.
- `fontsize=12, color='blue'`: Adjusts the font size and color of the annotation.

12.2.2 Adding Labels

Adding clear **labels** to the axes and title makes your plot more understandable.

```
python
```

```
# Create a plot
plt.plot(x, y)

# Add title and axis labels
plt.title('Customized    Plot    with    Labels',
fontsize=16)
plt.xlabel('X Axis Label', fontsize=14)
plt.ylabel('Y Axis Label', fontsize=14)

# Show the plot
plt.show()
```

◆ **Explanation**:

- `plt.title()`, `plt.xlabel()`, and `plt.ylabel()`:
  Adds a **title** and **axis labels** with custom font sizes.

12.2.3 Adding Legends

Legends are useful when plotting multiple datasets or lines. They help identify which data corresponds to which plot element.

```
python
```

```
# Create two lines with labels for the legend
plt.plot(x, y, label='Line 1', color='green')
```

143

```
plt.plot([1, 2, 3, 4, 5], [1, 2, 3, 4, 5],
label='Line 2', color='red', linestyle='--')

# Add title and labels
plt.title('Plot with Legends', fontsize=16)
plt.xlabel('X Axis', fontsize=12)
plt.ylabel('Y Axis', fontsize=12)

# Add a legend
plt.legend()

# Show the plot
plt.show()
```

◆ Explanation:

- `label='Line 1'` and `label='Line 2'`: Assigns labels to each line.
- `plt.legend()`: Displays the **legend** in the plot.

12.3 Making Plots Interactive with Widgets

Matplotlib plots are often static, but you can add **interactive elements** like sliders, buttons, and checkboxes using **widgets**. This allows users to dynamically adjust parameters and explore the data.

12.3.1 Using Widgets for Interactivity

We'll use the `matplotlib.widgets` module to add **sliders** for adjusting plot properties.

python

```python
import numpy as np
import matplotlib.pyplot as plt
from matplotlib.widgets import Slider

# Create a figure and axis
fig, ax = plt.subplots(figsize=(8, 6))
plt.subplots_adjust(bottom=0.25)

# Create some data
x = np.linspace(0, 10, 100)
y = np.sin(x)

# Plot the data
line, = plt.plot(x, y, label='Sine Wave')

# Add a slider to control the amplitude
axcolor = 'lightgoldenrodyellow'
ax_amplitude = plt.axes([0.25, 0.1, 0.65, 0.03],
facecolor=axcolor)
amplitude_slider    =    Slider(ax_amplitude,
'Amplitude', 0.1, 2.0, valinit=1)
```

```python
# Update function for the slider
def update(val):
    amplitude = amplitude_slider.val
    line.set_ydata(amplitude * np.sin(x))
    fig.canvas.draw_idle()

# Attach the slider to the update function
amplitude_slider.on_changed(update)

# Add title and labels
plt.title('Interactive Sine Wave', fontsize=16)
plt.xlabel('X Axis', fontsize=12)
plt.ylabel('Y Axis', fontsize=12)

# Show the plot
plt.show()
```

◆ Explanation:

- `Slider()`: Creates a **slider** widget that allows you to adjust the **amplitude** of the sine wave.
- `update(val)`: Updates the plot based on the slider's value, changing the **amplitude** of the sine wave.

12.3.2 Adding Multiple Widgets

You can add more widgets like buttons, checkboxes, or text inputs to control different aspects of the plot.

```python

from matplotlib.widgets import Button

# Create a button widget
ax_button = plt.axes([0.7, 0.025, 0.15, 0.075])
button    =    Button(ax_button,    'Reset',
color=axcolor, hovercolor='lightblue')

# Reset function for the button
def reset(event):
    amplitude_slider.reset()

# Attach the reset function to the button
button.on_clicked(reset)

# Show the plot with button
plt.show()
```

◆ **Explanation**:

- `Button()`: Creates a **button** that triggers the **reset** function when clicked.

12.4 Summary and Next Steps

In this chapter, we covered how to:

- **Customize plot appearance** with **fonts**, **colors**, and **markers** to improve the clarity and aesthetics of your visualizations.
- **Add annotations**, **labels**, and **legends** to make your plots more informative and readable.
- Make your plots **interactive** by adding **widgets** such as sliders and buttons, enabling users to explore the data dynamically.

Next Chapter: Creating Dashboards with Plotly and Dash

In the next chapter, we will explore how to build **interactive dashboards** using **Plotly** and **Dash**, where we can integrate multiple visualizations and add real-time data interactivity.

◆ **Key Takeaway**: Customizing plots in **Matplotlib** makes your visualizations more insightful and engaging. By adjusting fonts, colors, markers, and interactivity, you can create **clear, informative**, and **dynamic visualizations**. 🚀

4o mini

CHAPTER 13

Creating Dashboards with Dash

13.1 Introduction to Dash and Its Components

Dash is a powerful web application framework built on top of **Plotly** and **Flask**. It allows you to build highly **interactive, data-driven web dashboards** entirely in Python, without requiring advanced web development skills. Dashboards are a great way to **present data interactively**, allowing users to explore and manipulate the data through various **inputs** like dropdowns, sliders, and buttons.

Dashboards created with Dash are particularly useful for tasks such as:

- **Visualizing trends** in real-time data
- Creating **interactive reports**
- Building **business intelligence tools**

Dash simplifies the process of building interactive, web-based applications for data visualization. It allows you to create and deploy dashboards with just Python, making it an ideal choice for Python users working with data science and analytics.

Key Components of Dash:

- **Dash Components**: Pre-built interactive UI components like **dropdowns, sliders, graphs, buttons**, etc.
- **Dash Layout**: A structure for organizing the dashboard, composed of **HTML** and **interactive components**.
- **Dash Callbacks**: Python functions that update the dashboard dynamically in response to user input, such as a **click, selection**, or **slider change**.

13.2 Building Interactive Dashboards with Dash

13.2.1 Setting Up a Basic Dash App

To get started with Dash, you need to install the `dash` library if you haven't already:

bash

```
pip install dash
```

Next, you can create a basic **Dash app** with interactive elements. Here's an example of a simple dashboard that shows a plot and allows the user to interact with a slider to change the data:

python

```python
import dash
from dash import dcc, html
import plotly.express as px
from dash.dependencies import Input, Output

# Create Dash app
app = dash.Dash(__name__)

# Sample dataset (Iris dataset)
df = px.data.iris()

# Dash app layout
app.layout = html.Div([
    html.H1("Interactive Dash Dashboard"),

    # Dropdown to select the species
    dcc.Dropdown(
        id='species-dropdown',
        options=[
            {'label': species, 'value': species}
for species in df['species'].unique()
        ],
        value='setosa',  # Default value
        style={'width': '50%'}
```

```
    ),

    # Graph for the scatter plot
    dcc.Graph(id='scatter-plot'),

    # Slider for controlling the marker size
    dcc.Slider(
        id='size-slider',
        min=5,
        max=30,
        step=1,
        value=10,   # Default value
        marks={i: str(i) for i in range(5, 31,
5)}
    )
])


# Callback to update the plot based on dropdown
and slider input
@app.callback(
    Output('scatter-plot', 'figure'),
    [Input('species-dropdown', 'value'),
     Input('size-slider', 'value')]
)
def update_plot(selected_species, marker_size):
    filtered_df    =    df[df['species']    ==
selected_species]
```

```
    fig          =          px.scatter(filtered_df,
x='sepal_width',              y='sepal_length',
color='species',
                    size='petal_length',
size_max=marker_size)
    return fig


# Run the app
if __name__ == '__main__':
    app.run_server(debug=True)
```

◆ **Explanation**:

- `dcc.Dropdown()`: Creates a dropdown to select the species.

- `dcc.Graph()`: Adds a graph to the layout where the scatter plot will be shown.

- `dcc.Slider()`: Adds a slider to adjust the size of the markers in the scatter plot.

- `@app.callback()`: Links the dropdown and slider inputs to the graph, making the plot dynamically update when either is changed.

13.2.2 Customizing Dashboards with Multiple Components

In Dash, you can use a wide range of pre-built components to customize your dashboard. Components can be combined in different ways to create multi-page layouts or interactive interfaces.

python

```
app.layout = html.Div([
    html.H1("Advanced Dashboard Example"),

    html.Div([
        dcc.Dropdown(
            id='x-axis-dropdown',
            options=[{'label':  col,  'value':
col} for col in df.columns],
            value='sepal_width',
        ),
        dcc.Dropdown(
            id='y-axis-dropdown',
            options=[{'label':  col,  'value':
col} for col in df.columns],
            value='sepal_length',
        ),
    ],  style={'display':  'flex',  'justify-
content': 'space-between'}),

    dcc.Graph(id='dynamic-graph')
])

@app.callback(
    Output('dynamic-graph', 'figure'),
```

```
[Input('x-axis-dropdown', 'value'),
    Input('y-axis-dropdown', 'value')]
)
def update_dynamic_graph(x_axis, y_axis):
    fig = px.scatter(df, x=x_axis, y=y_axis,
color='species')
    return fig
```

✦ Explanation:

- `dcc.Dropdown()`: Adds dropdowns to choose which columns of the dataset to plot on the x and y axes.
- **Flexbox layout**: Organizes the dropdowns in a responsive layout.

13.3 Deploying Dash Dashboards for Web Use

Once you've created a dashboard, you can deploy it to the web for others to access. Dash applications can be deployed easily on **cloud platforms** like **Heroku**, **AWS**, or **Google Cloud**. In this section, we'll look at how to deploy your Dash app to Heroku, a popular cloud platform for Python applications.

13.3.1 Preparing the App for Deployment

To deploy your Dash app to Heroku, you need to prepare a few key files:

1. **requirements.txt**: This file contains all the Python dependencies for the app.

```bash

dash
plotly
pandas
```

2. **Procfile**: This file tells Heroku how to run your Dash app.

```bash

web: python app.py
```

3. **runtime.txt** (optional): Specify the Python version you want Heroku to use.

```bash

python-3.8.12
```

13.3.2 Deploying to Heroku

- First, create a **Heroku account** and install the **Heroku CLI** on your system.
- Initialize a **git repository** in your project folder:

```bash

git init
git add .
git commit -m "Initial commit"
```

- Log in to Heroku using the command line:

```bash

heroku login
```

- Create a Heroku app:

```bash

heroku create your-app-name
```

- Push your code to Heroku:

```bash

git push heroku master
```

157

- Once deployed, Heroku provides a **URL** where your Dash app will be hosted.

13.4 Summary and Next Steps

In this chapter, we:

- Introduced **Dash** and its key components for building interactive dashboards, including **layout**, **components**, and **callbacks**.
- Walked through building a simple Dash dashboard with interactive elements such as **dropdowns**, **sliders**, and **graphs**.
- Covered how to **deploy** Dash applications for web use using **Heroku**.

Next Chapter: Advanced Dashboards with Multiple Pages and Real-Time Data

In the next chapter, we will explore how to build **multi-page dashboards** and integrate **real-time data updates** into your Dash applications, allowing you to create more sophisticated data visualizations.

✦ **Key Takeaway**: Dash empowers you to create **interactive** and **dynamic dashboards** using just Python. With its simplicity and flexibility, Dash is ideal for visualizing complex data and deploying web-based interactive applications. 🚀

CHAPTER 14

Working with Multiple Axes and Subplots

14.1 Creating Complex Plots with Multiple Axes

When dealing with multiple variables or datasets, it can often be useful to display them in the same plot for easy comparison. **Multiple axes** allow you to create plots where different variables share the same x-axis or y-axis, or even create independent axes that showcase various dimensions of your data. Matplotlib provides several ways to customize **multiple axes** within a single figure.

14.1.1 Basic Multiple Axes with Matplotlib

To create complex plots with **multiple axes**, you can use `plt.subplots()`, which allows you to specify the number of rows and columns in your figure and create a grid of subplots.

```python
python

import matplotlib.pyplot as plt
```

```python
import numpy as np

# Create some data
x = np.linspace(0, 10, 100)
y1 = np.sin(x)
y2 = np.cos(x)

# Create a 1x2 subplot grid
fig, (ax1, ax2) = plt.subplots(1, 2, figsize=(12, 6))

# Plot data on the first axis
ax1.plot(x, y1, color='blue', label='Sine Wave')
ax1.set_title('Sine Wave')
ax1.set_xlabel('X Axis')
ax1.set_ylabel('Y Axis')
ax1.legend()

# Plot data on the second axis
ax2.plot(x, y2, color='red', label='Cosine Wave')
ax2.set_title('Cosine Wave')
ax2.set_xlabel('X Axis')
ax2.set_ylabel('Y Axis')
ax2.legend()

# Show the plot
plt.tight_layout()
plt.show()
```

◆ **Explanation**:

- `plt.subplots(1, 2)`: Creates a **1x2 grid** of subplots, where `ax1` and `ax2` represent the individual axes.
- `ax1.plot(x, y1)`: Plots the **sine wave** on the first axis (`ax1`), and `ax2.plot(x, y2)` plots the **cosine wave** on the second axis (`ax2`).
- `tight_layout()`: Adjusts the layout to ensure the subplots fit within the figure area without overlap.

12.1.2 Sharing Axes Between Plots

Sometimes you might want to share the same x-axis or y-axis between subplots for consistency and comparison. This can be achieved by setting the `sharex` and `sharey` parameters.

python

```
fig, (ax1, ax2) = plt.subplots(1, 2, figsize=(12,
6), sharex=True, sharey=True)

# Plot data on the first axis
ax1.plot(x, y1, color='blue', label='Sine Wave')
ax1.set_title('Sine Wave')

# Plot data on the second axis
```

```
ax2.plot(x,    y2,    color='red',    label='Cosine
Wave')
ax2.set_title('Cosine Wave')

plt.tight_layout()
plt.show()
```

◆ **Explanation**:

- `sharex=True, sharey=True`: This ensures that both
  `ax1` and `ax2` share the same **x-axis** and **y-axis**, making
  comparison easier.

12.2 Using Subplots for Data Comparison

Subplots are a great way to compare multiple datasets or
visualize multiple aspects of the same dataset within the
same figure. With Matplotlib, you can create **subplots** with
different types of visualizations, such as histograms, line
plots, and scatter plots, to facilitate comparison.

12.2.1 Creating Multiple Plots for Comparison

Let's say you have multiple distributions of data (e.g., sales
in different regions), and you want to compare them side by
side:

```python
python

# Create sample data
region_1 = np.random.normal(100, 10, 1000)
region_2 = np.random.normal(120, 15, 1000)

# Create a 1x2 subplot grid
fig, (ax1, ax2) = plt.subplots(1, 2, figsize=(12, 6))

# Create histograms for comparison
ax1.hist(region_1, bins=30, color='skyblue', edgecolor='black', alpha=0.7)
ax1.set_title('Region 1 Sales Distribution')

ax2.hist(region_2, bins=30, color='salmon', edgecolor='black', alpha=0.7)
ax2.set_title('Region 2 Sales Distribution')

plt.tight_layout()
plt.show()
```

◆ Explanation:

- Two **histograms** are created side by side for **Region 1** and **Region 2**.
- `plt.tight_layout()`: Adjusts the space between subplots to avoid overlap and improve presentation.

164

12.3 Advanced Multi-Axis Visualizations with Seaborn and Plotly

12.3.1 Using Seaborn for Multi-Axis Plots

Seaborn provides high-level functions to quickly generate complex plots. It supports creating **facet grids** and **multiple plots** with ease.

For example, using **Seaborn's FacetGrid**, you can create multiple subplots based on categories within the dataset:

python

```python
import seaborn as sns

# Load the tips dataset from Seaborn
df = sns.load_dataset('tips')

# Create a FacetGrid of scatter plots, comparing
day and sex
g = sns.FacetGrid(df, col="day", row="sex")
g.map(sns.scatterplot, "total_bill", "tip")

plt.show()
```

♦ **Explanation**:

- `sns.FacetGrid()`: Creates a grid of subplots, one for each combination of `day` and `sex` categories.
- `g.map()`: Maps a scatter plot onto each facet of the grid.

12.3.2 Advanced Multi-Axis Plots with Plotly

Plotly's flexibility allows you to easily create **multiple axes** and **subplots** with interactive features. Here's how you can create multiple plots and add interactivity:

python

```python
import plotly.graph_objects as go

# Create a subplot with 2 rows and 1 column
fig = go.Figure()

# Add a line plot in the first subplot (top)
fig.add_trace(go.Scatter(x=x,                y=y1,
mode='lines', name='Sine Wave'))

# Add a bar plot in the second subplot (bottom)
fig.add_trace(go.Bar(x=x,    y=np.abs(np.sin(x)),
name='Abs(Sine)'))
```

```
# Update layout to adjust the subplot titles and
axes
fig.update_layout(
    title='Multi-Axis    Visualization    with
Plotly',
    grid=dict(rows=2, columns=1),
    xaxis=dict(title="X Axis"),
    yaxis=dict(title="Y Axis")
)

fig.show()
```

◈ **Explanation**:

- `go.Figure()`: Creates a **Plotly figure**.
- `add_trace()`: Adds **multiple types of plots** (scatter for line and bar for bar chart).
- `update_layout()`: Customizes the layout, including setting titles and axes for each subplot.

12.4 Customizing Multi-Axis Plots

In some cases, you may want to have different **y-axes** for each plot, such as when comparing datasets with different units or scales. Matplotlib allows you to add **secondary y-axes** to a plot.

12.4.1 Creating Multi-Axis Plots in Matplotlib

python

```
fig, ax1 = plt.subplots(figsize=(10, 6))

# First plot with primary y-axis
ax1.plot(x,    y1,   color='green',   label='Sine
Wave')
ax1.set_xlabel('X Axis')
ax1.set_ylabel('Sine Wave', color='green')

# Create a second y-axis on the same plot
ax2 = ax1.twinx()
ax2.plot(x,   y2,   color='orange',   label='Cosine
Wave')
ax2.set_ylabel('Cosine Wave', color='orange')

# Add a title
plt.title('Sine and Cosine Waves with Multiple Y
Axes')

plt.show()
```

◆ Explanation:

- `ax1.twinx()`: Creates a **second y-axis** that shares the same x-axis but has its own scale.
- The **sine wave** is plotted on the left y-axis, and the **cosine wave** is plotted on the right y-axis.

12.5 Summary and Next Steps

In this chapter, we:

- Learned how to create **complex plots with multiple axes** using Matplotlib, including how to share axes between subplots.
- Explored how to use **subplots** for easy comparison of multiple datasets.
- Covered **advanced multi-axis visualizations** using Seaborn's **FacetGrid** and Plotly's **subplots** and **multi-axis plots**.
- Demonstrated how to **customize multi-axis plots** for clearer comparisons of different data.

Next Chapter: Creating Interactive Dashboards with Plotly and Dash

In the next chapter, we will explore **interactive dashboards** with **Plotly** and **Dash**, showing how to create real-time data visualizations and build complex, interactive web applications.

♦ **Key Takeaway**: Multi-axis and subplot visualizations allow you to display and compare multiple datasets or variables efficiently. These techniques are powerful tools for **data analysis** and **visual storytelling**. 🚀

CHAPTER 15

Animated Visualizations

12.1 Introduction to Creating Animated Plots with Matplotlib

Animations are a powerful way to convey dynamic data changes over time. Instead of static plots, animated visualizations allow you to showcase the evolution of data, trends, or processes as they unfold. This is particularly useful in scenarios like **time series data**, **simulations**, or **data that changes dynamically** over time, such as weather patterns, stock prices, or traffic flow.

In Matplotlib, animations are created by updating the plot's elements, such as lines, markers, and annotations, within a loop. The `FuncAnimation` class is used to animate plots in Matplotlib.

12.1.1 Basic Animation with Matplotlib

Here's a simple example of how to animate a sine wave to visualize changes over time:

```python
python

import matplotlib.pyplot as plt
import numpy as np
from matplotlib.animation import FuncAnimation

# Set up the figure, the axis, and the plot
element
fig, ax = plt.subplots()
x = np.linspace(0, 2 * np.pi, 100)
y = np.sin(x)

line, = ax.plot(x, y, color='blue')

# Define the update function for the animation
def update(frame):
    line.set_ydata(np.sin(x + frame / 10))    #
Update the y-data
    return line,

# Create the animation
ani = FuncAnimation(fig, update, frames=100,
interval=50, blit=True)

# Display the plot
plt.title("Animated Sine Wave")
plt.xlabel("X Axis")
plt.ylabel("Y Axis")
plt.show()
```

✦ Explanation:

- `FuncAnimation()`: This is the core function for creating animations. It takes the figure, update function, frame count, and interval between frames as inputs.
- `update()`: This function updates the data of the plot at each frame. In this case, the y-values of the sine wave are shifted by a small amount to create the animation effect.
- `blit=True`: This option optimizes the drawing by only redrawing the elements that have changed in each frame.

12.1.2 Customizing Animation Speed and Style

You can control the speed and style of your animation by adjusting the **frame rate** and **frame data**.

python

```
# Modify animation speed by changing interval
ani = FuncAnimation(fig, update, frames=200,
interval=20, blit=True)

# Save the animation to a file (optional)
ani.save('sine_wave_animation.gif',
writer='imagemagick')
```

✦ Explanation:

- `interval=20`: Adjusts the interval between frames (in milliseconds). Lower values make the animation faster, while higher values slow it down.
- `ani.save()`: Saves the animation as a `.gif` or `.mp4` file for sharing or embedding.

12.2 Building Animations to Visualize Time-Based Changes

Animations are ideal for visualizing **time-based data**, as they show how the data evolves over a continuous time period. In this section, we'll create an animation to visualize how a stock price changes over time.

12.2.1 Example: Animating Stock Price Changes

Let's say we have data representing a stock price over time. We can create an animation to visualize the stock price fluctuations.

python

```
import pandas as pd
import matplotlib.pyplot as plt
from matplotlib.animation import FuncAnimation
```

```python
# Generate random stock price data over 100 days
np.random.seed(0)
days = np.arange(1, 101)
prices = np.cumsum(np.random.randn(100) * 5 + 50)
# Simulated stock price

fig, ax = plt.subplots()
ax.set_xlim(0, 100)
ax.set_ylim(min(prices) - 10, max(prices) + 10)

line, = ax.plot([], [], lw=2)
ax.set_title('Stock Price Over Time')
ax.set_xlabel('Days')
ax.set_ylabel('Stock Price ($)')

# Initialization function: plots the background
of each frame
def init():
    line.set_data([], [])
    return line,

# Update function: updates the plot data for each
frame
def update(frame):
    line.set_data(days[:frame], prices[:frame])
    return line,

# Create the animation
```

```
ani = FuncAnimation(fig, update, frames=100,
init_func=init, blit=True, interval=100)

# Show the animation
plt.show()
```

◆ **Explanation**:

- `np.cumsum()`: Generates cumulative sums to simulate stock price movements.
- `update()`: The function updates the plot by drawing the stock price up to the current day (`frame`).
- The `init()` function initializes the plot with an empty line.

12.3 Plotly Animation for Interactive Data Exploration

While Matplotlib is excellent for static and simple animations, **Plotly** allows for **interactive animations**. Plotly animations are great for **exploring changes over time**, with the added benefit of **hover features**, **zooming**, and **panning**.

12.3.1 Creating Interactive Animations with Plotly

Plotly's animation capabilities allow users to create interactive charts that update based on a **time variable** or **data sequence**.

Here's an example of creating an animated scatter plot to show how data points evolve over time:

```python
python

import plotly.express as px
import pandas as pd
import numpy as np

# Create a sample dataset with time-based changes
time = np.arange(1, 101)
x = np.sin(time * 0.1) * 10
y = np.cos(time * 0.1) * 10

df = pd.DataFrame({'Time': time, 'X': x, 'Y': y})

# Create an animated scatter plot
fig    =    px.scatter(df,    x='X',    y='Y',
animation_frame='Time',
               title="Interactive    Animated
Scatter Plot",
               range_x=[-12,   12],   range_y=[-
12, 12])
```

```
# Show the plot
fig.show()
```

◆ Explanation:

- `px.scatter()`: Creates an **animated scatter plot** where the data points change over time.
- `animation_frame='Time'`: Specifies that the animation will update with the `Time` variable.
- **Interactive Features**: The Plotly plot allows for **hovering**, **zooming**, and **panning** to explore data more interactively.

12.3.2 Customizing Plotly Animations

Plotly also allows you to **customize** the appearance of animated plots, such as adjusting the speed, adding transitions, or controlling the appearance of data points.

```python
fig.update_layout(
    updatemenus=[dict(
        type="buttons",           showactive=False,
buttons=[dict(label="Play",    method="animate",
args=[None,          dict(frame=dict(duration=100,
redraw=True),  fromcurrent=True)])])])
```

```
fig.show()
```

✦ Explanation:

- `updatemenus`: Adds interactive controls (e.g., a **play button**) for the user to control the animation.
- `duration=100`: Adjusts the speed of the animation, where lower values make it faster.

12.4 Summary and Next Steps

In this chapter, we:

- Introduced **animated visualizations** as a way to showcase time-based changes and dynamic data.
- Created simple animations using **Matplotlib** for static plots and time-series data.
- Explored **Plotly** for **interactive animations** that allow users to explore data dynamically.

Next Chapter: Visualizing Networks and Graphs

In the next chapter, we will explore how to visualize **networks** and **graphs**, focusing on how to represent relationships and connections between entities using visual tools like **network diagrams** and **graph visualizations**.

◆ **Key Takeaway**: Animated visualizations breathe life into data, allowing you to demonstrate how it evolves over time. **Matplotlib** and **Plotly** offer powerful animation tools, with **Matplotlib** providing simple animations and **Plotly** enabling interactive, web-based exploration. 🚀

PART 4

DATA VISUALIZATION FOR BUSINESS INTELLIGENCE

CHAPTER 16

Visualizing Financial Data

16.1 Best Practices for Visualizing Stock Prices, Revenue, and Financial Reports

Financial data is at the core of **business intelligence** (BI) and decision-making. For executives, analysts, and decision-makers, **clear visualizations** of financial metrics like **stock prices**, **revenue**, and **profit margins** are essential to understanding business performance, forecasting trends, and making data-driven decisions.

Here are some best practices for visualizing financial data:

16.1.1 Choosing the Right Visualizations

- **Line Charts**: Use **line charts** to track the **time series** of stock prices, revenue growth, or market trends. They allow you to observe fluctuations, trends, and patterns.
- **Candlestick Charts**: Commonly used in **stock market analysis**, candlestick charts provide detailed information about **price movements** over time, including **open**, **high**, **low**, and **close** values.

- **Bar and Column Charts**: These are ideal for comparing **financial performance** across different time periods or categories, such as monthly revenue or quarterly profits.
- **Pie Charts**: Use **pie charts** for visualizing **market share**, **asset distribution**, or **portfolio breakdowns**.
- **Heatmaps**: Use **heatmaps** for **correlation analysis** of financial metrics, helping to identify relationships between variables (e.g., **stock performance** vs. **interest rates**).

16.1.2 Maintaining Simplicity

While it might be tempting to include multiple variables or complex metrics, remember that financial visualizations must be **simple**, **clear**, and **actionable**. Avoid clutter and focus on presenting the data in a way that leads to **insightful business decisions**.

16.2 Creating Candlestick Charts and Stock Price Trends with Plotly

Candlestick charts are essential tools for **stock market analysis**. They show the price movements over time for a particular asset, with each candlestick representing a specific time period. The **body** of the candlestick shows the **open** and **close** prices, while the **wicks** show the **high** and **low** prices during that period.

16.2.1 Basic Candlestick Chart Using Plotly

Plotly provides an easy way to create **interactive candlestick charts** with its built-in **plotly.graph_objects** library.

python

```python
import plotly.graph_objects as go
import pandas as pd

# Sample stock data (dates, open, high, low, close)
data = {
    'Date': ['2023-01-01', '2023-01-02', '2023-01-03', '2023-01-04'],
    'Open': [100, 102, 105, 107],
    'High': [105, 106, 110, 108],
    'Low': [99, 100, 103, 105],
    'Close': [104, 105, 107, 106]
}

df = pd.DataFrame(data)

# Create the candlestick chart
```

```
fig                                                        =
go.Figure(data=[go.Candlestick(x=df['Date'],
                   open=df['Open'],
high=df['High'],
                   low=df['Low'],
close=df['Close'])])

fig.update_layout(title="Candlestick        Chart
Example",
                   xaxis_title="Date",
                   yaxis_title="Stock Price ($)")

fig.show()
```

◆ **Explanation**:

- `go.Candlestick()`: Creates the **candlestick chart**, using `open`, `high`, `low`, and `close` values from the dataset.
- `fig.update_layout()`: Customizes the chart title and axis labels.

16.2.2 Customizing Candlestick Charts

You can customize candlestick charts to add **color** and make them more intuitive for business decision-makers. For instance, you can color the **up days** (close > open) green and the **down days** (close < open) red.

185

```python
python

# Customize candlestick colors
fig                                            =
go.Figure(data=[go.Candlestick(x=df['Date'],
                open=df['Open'],
high=df['High'],
                low=df['Low'],
close=df['Close'],
                increasing_line_color='green',
decreasing_line_color='red')])

fig.update_layout(title="Customized  Candlestick
Chart",
                xaxis_title="Date",
                yaxis_title="Stock Price ($)")

fig.show()
```

◆ **Explanation**:

- `increasing_line_color='green'` and `decreasing_line_color='red'`: Colors the **up days** green and **down days** red, making it easier for users to identify positive and negative price movements.

16.2.3 Creating Stock Price Trends with Line Charts

Line charts are perfect for visualizing **stock price trends** over time. They help to identify **overall trends, volatility,** and **patterns** in a more continuous way.

```python
# Plot stock price trend using a line chart
fig = go.Figure(data=[go.Scatter(x=df['Date'],
y=df['Close'],    mode='lines',    name='Stock
Price')])

fig.update_layout(title="Stock Price Trend",
                  xaxis_title="Date",
                  yaxis_title="Stock Price ($)")

fig.show()
```

◆ **Explanation**:

- go.Scatter(): Creates a **line chart** using the Close price to visualize the **stock price trend** over time.

16.3 Customizing Financial Visualizations for Decision-Makers

When presenting financial data to decision-makers, it's important to ensure that the visualizations are not only clear but also **insightful** and **actionable**. Here are a few ways to customize financial visualizations for business use:

16.3.1 Adding Annotations

Annotations are particularly useful for drawing attention to significant events in your financial data, such as **earnings announcements, mergers,** or **stock price spikes**.

python

```
fig                                    =
go.Figure(data=[go.Candlestick(x=df['Date'],
                open=df['Open'],
high=df['High'],
                low=df['Low'],
close=df['Close'])])

# Adding annotations for significant events
fig.add_annotation(x='2023-01-03',         y=107,
text='Earnings      Report',      showarrow=True,
arrowhead=2)

fig.update_layout(title="Candlestick  Chart  with
Annotations",
                xaxis_title="Date",
```

```
                     yaxis_title="Stock Price ($)")
```

```
fig.show()
```

◆ **Explanation**:

- `fig.add_annotation()`: Adds an annotation to the chart, marking a specific date and price level.
- **Annotations** are particularly helpful for **business decision-makers** to correlate stock price movements with **events** or **news**.

16.3.2 Using Interactive Dashboards

To provide a more comprehensive view of financial data, you can use **Dash** to create interactive dashboards that integrate candlestick charts, line charts, and other financial visualizations. These dashboards allow decision-makers to interact with the data and explore different time periods, stock comparisons, or financial metrics.

```python
```

```
import dash
from dash import dcc, html
import plotly.graph_objects as go

# Sample Dash app
```

```python
app = dash.Dash(__name__)

app.layout = html.Div([
    html.H1("Interactive Financial Dashboard"),

    dcc.Graph(id='stock-price-chart',
              figure=fig),  # Assuming fig is the
Plotly figure created above

    html.Label("Select Time Period:"),
    dcc.Dropdown(
        id='time-period-dropdown',
        options=[
            {'label': '1 Month', 'value': '1M'},
            {'label': '3 Months', 'value':
'3M'},
            {'label': '6 Months', 'value': '6M'}
        ],
        value='1M'  # Default value
    )
])

# Callback to update the chart based on selected
time period (Example)
@app.callback(
    dash.dependencies.Output('stock-price-
chart', 'figure'),
    [dash.dependencies.Input('time-period-
dropdown', 'value')]
```

```
)
def update_chart(time_period):
    # Modify the data based on the selected time
period
    return fig  # Update the figure based on the
selected time period

# Run the app
if __name__ == '__main__':
    app.run_server(debug=True)
```

◈ Explanation:

- **Dash** is used to create an interactive **financial dashboard**, where users can **select time periods** (like 1 month, 3 months) to adjust the data displayed in the charts.
- This interactive approach allows decision-makers to explore **different segments** of financial data with ease.

16.4 Summary and Next Steps

In this chapter, we:

- Explored best practices for visualizing **financial data**, such as **stock prices, revenue**, and **financial reports**.

- Learned how to create **candlestick charts** and **stock price trend visualizations** using **Plotly**.

- Discussed how to **customize** financial visualizations for **business decision-makers**, including **annotations** and **interactive dashboards**.

Next Chapter: Advanced Visualizations for Business Analytics

In the next chapter, we will delve into **advanced visualization techniques** for **business analytics**, including **geospatial visualizations**, **network graphs**, and **time-series forecasting** visualizations for deeper insights.

◆ **Key Takeaway**: Financial visualizations, especially **candlestick charts** and **stock trends**, are essential for decision-makers to interpret complex financial data. **Plotly** provides powerful tools for creating **interactive** and **customized visualizations** that can guide informed, data-driven business decisions. 🚀

CHAPTER 17

Visualizing Customer Data

17.1 Visualizing Customer Segmentation and Demographics

Visualizing **customer segmentation** and **demographics** is crucial for businesses to understand their customer base and create targeted strategies. By grouping customers based on similar characteristics, businesses can tailor their marketing efforts, products, and services to different groups.

17.1.1 Customer Segmentation

Customer segmentation involves dividing a customer base into distinct groups based on common characteristics such as **age**, **location**, **purchase behavior**, or **spending habits**. Visualizing this data allows businesses to identify trends and make informed decisions.

Here's an example of visualizing customer segmentation using a **scatter plot** to show spending and age distribution:

python

193

```python
import plotly.express as px
import pandas as pd
import numpy as np

# Sample customer segmentation data
np.random.seed(0)
n = 200
age = np.random.randint(18, 70, n)
spending = np.random.randint(100, 2000, n)
segment = np.random.choice(['Young', 'Middle-Aged', 'Senior'], n)

df = pd.DataFrame({
    'Age': age,
    'Spending': spending,
    'Segment': segment
})

# Scatter plot to visualize customer segmentation
fig = px.scatter(df, x='Age', y='Spending',
color='Segment', title="Customer Segmentation by
Age and Spending")
fig.show()
```

♦ Explanation:

- `px.scatter()`: Creates a **scatter plot** where customers are divided by age and spending.

- `color='Segment'`: Uses color to differentiate between customer segments (e.g., Young, Middle-Aged, Senior).
- This type of plot helps identify trends, such as which segments spend more or are concentrated in certain age groups.

17.1.2 Demographic Breakdown

A **demographic breakdown** visualizes how different groups of customers (e.g., by age, gender, or region) are distributed. You can use bar charts, pie charts, or histograms to display this information.

python

```python
# Bar chart for gender distribution
gender = np.random.choice(['Male', 'Female'], n)
df['Gender'] = gender

fig = px.bar(df, x='Gender', title="Customer Gender Distribution", color='Gender')
fig.show()
```

◆ **Explanation**:

- `px.bar()`: Creates a **bar chart** to display the gender distribution of customers.

195

- Visualizing **demographics** helps businesses understand their customer base's characteristics, which can inform marketing and product decisions.

17.2 Creating Cohort Analysis and Retention Curves

Cohort analysis is a powerful tool for understanding how different groups of customers behave over time. Typically, cohorts are groups of customers who share a common characteristic or experience, such as signing up for a service in the same month.

17.2.1 Creating Cohort Analysis

A **cohort analysis** chart helps track customer retention, repeat purchases, or engagement over time. Here's how to create a **retention curve** using a cohort analysis:

python

```
import matplotlib.pyplot as plt
import numpy as np

# Simulated cohort retention data
```

```
cohorts = np.array([[1000, 850, 700, 650],
                    [1000, 780, 650, 600],
                    [1000, 900, 850, 800]])

# Create a retention curve for each cohort
fig, ax = plt.subplots(figsize=(10, 6))

for cohort in cohorts:
    ax.plot(range(1, len(cohort)+1), cohort,
marker='o',                            label=f'Cohort
{cohorts.tolist().index(cohort)+1}')

# Add titles and labels
ax.set_title("Cohort Retention Over Time")
ax.set_xlabel("Months Since Signup")
ax.set_ylabel("Customers Retained")
ax.legend()

plt.show()
```

✦ Explanation:

- The **cohorts** represent customers who signed up in different months, and each row shows the number of customers retained in subsequent months.

- `ax.plot()`: Plots the **retention curve** for each cohort to visualize how many customers continue using the service over time.

This type of plot helps identify how retention rates vary between cohorts, guiding improvements in customer retention strategies.

17.2.2 Customizing Cohort Analysis

Customizing your cohort analysis with **interactive tools** like **Plotly** enables decision-makers to explore different time periods or cohorts dynamically.

python

```python
import plotly.express as px

# Creating cohort data for Plotly
cohort_data = {
    'Cohort': ['January', 'February', 'March'],
    'Month 1': [1000, 1000, 1000],
    'Month 2': [850, 780, 900],
    'Month 3': [700, 650, 850],
    'Month 4': [650, 600, 800]
}

df_cohort = pd.DataFrame(cohort_data)

# Create interactive cohort retention plot with
Plotly
fig     =      px.line(df_cohort,      x='Cohort',
y=df_cohort.columns[1:],
```

```
            title="Customer    Retention    Over
Time by Cohort", markers=True)
fig.show()
```

◆ **Explanation**:

- `px.line()`: Creates an **interactive line plot** that shows customer retention for each cohort over time.
- The **interactive features** of Plotly make it easier to explore data and understand patterns.

17.3 Mapping Customer Journeys Using Sankey Diagrams

A **Sankey diagram** is a great way to visualize customer journeys, especially when you need to show how users move between different states or actions in a process. Sankey diagrams can be used to represent **user flows**, such as the path customers take through your website, conversion funnels, or different stages of the customer lifecycle.

17.3.1 Creating Sankey Diagrams with Plotly

Plotly makes it easy to create **interactive Sankey diagrams** that help visualize how users move from one stage to

199

another. For instance, you can map how users progress through different stages of your **sales funnel** (e.g., from initial interest to purchase).

```python
import plotly.graph_objects as go

# Example of customer journey stages
stages = ['Visited Website', 'Signed Up', 'Made
a Purchase', 'Returned for Repeat Purchase']
values = [500, 300, 150, 50]  # Customers at each
stage

# Create Sankey diagram
fig = go.Figure(go.Sankey(
    node=dict(
        pad=15,
        thickness=20,
        line=dict(color="black", width=0.5),
        label=stages
    ),
    link=dict(
        source=[0, 1, 2],
        target=[1, 2, 3],
        value=values
    )
))
```

```
fig.update_layout(title_text="Customer    Journey
Flow", font_size=10)
fig.show()
```

◆ **Explanation**:

- `stages`: These are the **steps** in the customer journey.
- `link`: Defines the connections between the stages, with `source` and `target` indicating where the flow begins and ends, and `value` representing the number of customers.
- **Sankey diagrams** help you visually track how customers move through different stages of your funnel and identify potential drop-off points.

17.3.2 Customizing Sankey Diagrams

Sankey diagrams can be further customized to reflect more complex user flows and customer interactions, such as integrating **multiple funnels** or using **color coding** for different customer segments.

```
python
```

```
# Modify Sankey diagram with custom colors and
additional details
fig = go.Figure(go.Sankey(
    node=dict(
```

```
        pad=15,
        thickness=20,
        line=dict(color="black", width=0.5),
        label=stages,
        color=["#1f77b4", "#ff7f0e", "#2ca02c",
"#d62728"]  # Custom colors
    ),
    link=dict(
        source=[0, 1, 2],
        target=[1, 2, 3],
        value=values,
        color=["blue", "orange", "green"]    #
Custom link colors
    )
))

fig.update_layout(title_text="Customer    Journey
Flow with Custom Colors", font_size=10)
fig.show()
```

◆ Explanation:

- color: Customizes the **color** of the nodes and links to make the diagram more visually distinct and aligned with your branding or customer segments.

17.4 Summary and Next Steps

In this chapter, we:

- Explored how to visualize **customer segmentation** and **demographics** to gain insights into customer behaviors.
- Learned how to create **cohort analysis** charts and **retention curves** to track customer behavior over time.
- Built **Sankey diagrams** to map **customer journeys** and visualize flows between different stages of a process, such as a sales funnel.

Next Chapter: Advanced Data Visualizations for Marketing Analytics

In the next chapter, we will explore **advanced data visualizations** for **marketing analytics**, such as **conversion funnel visualizations**, **email campaign tracking**, and **customer lifetime value visualizations**.

◆ **Key Takeaway**: Visualizing **customer data** through segmentation, cohort analysis, and Sankey diagrams helps businesses better understand **customer behaviors**, improve **customer retention**, and optimize **marketing strategies** for better engagement. 🚀

CHAPTER 18

Sales and Marketing Data Visualizations

18.1 Creating Sales Performance Dashboards

Sales performance dashboards are essential for tracking the **health** of a business. They provide a quick and comprehensive view of key sales metrics like **total sales**, **sales by region**, **sales growth**, and **sales targets**. By visualizing sales performance, businesses can monitor trends, identify bottlenecks, and make data-driven decisions.

17.1.1 Building a Sales Dashboard with Plotly

To create a **dynamic sales performance dashboard**, we can use **Plotly Dash** to display multiple sales metrics in an interactive format. Here's how to set up a simple dashboard with **total sales**, **sales by region**, and **sales growth**.

python

```
import dash
from dash import dcc, html
```

```python
import plotly.express as px
import pandas as pd
import numpy as np

# Create a sample sales dataset
np.random.seed(0)
dates = pd.date_range('2023-01-01', periods=12,
freq='M')
sales = np.random.randint(1000, 5000, 12)
regions = ['North', 'South', 'East', 'West']
sales_by_region                =               {region:
np.random.randint(1000, 2000, 12) for region in
regions}

df_sales = pd.DataFrame({
    'Date': dates,
    'Sales': sales
})

df_region_sales = pd.DataFrame({
    'Date': dates,
    'North': sales_by_region['North'],
    'South': sales_by_region['South'],
    'East': sales_by_region['East'],
    'West': sales_by_region['West']
})

# Create Dash app
app = dash.Dash(__name__)
```

```
app.layout = html.Div([
    html.H1("Sales Performance Dashboard"),

    # Sales trend graph
    dcc.Graph(
        id='sales-trend',
        figure=px.line(df_sales,        x='Date',
y='Sales', title="Monthly Sales Trend")
    ),

    # Sales by region bar chart
    dcc.Graph(
        id='sales-region',
        figure=px.bar(df_region_sales, x='Date',
y=df_region_sales.columns[1:],
                      title="Sales  by  Region",
barmode='group')
    )
])

if __name__ == '__main__':
    app.run_server(debug=True)
```

◆ **Explanation**:

- **Dash App**: The app consists of multiple plots, such as a **line chart** showing monthly sales trends (`sales-trend`) and a **bar chart** showing sales by region (`sales-region`).

- **Plotly**: The `px.line()` and `px.bar()` functions help visualize sales performance.

17.1.2 Customizing the Dashboard for Business Needs

To make the dashboard more business-specific, you can add **filters** to interactively adjust the data (e.g., by selecting a particular region or date range), giving users more flexibility to explore the data.

17.2 Visualizing Campaign Performance: Conversion Rates and ROI

For marketing teams, tracking campaign performance is critical. Understanding **conversion rates**, **customer acquisition**, and **ROI** helps marketers assess the effectiveness of their campaigns and allocate resources efficiently.

17.2.1 Conversion Rates Visualization

The **conversion rate** is the percentage of visitors who take a desired action (e.g., making a purchase, signing up for a service). Visualizing the conversion rate over time allows businesses to evaluate campaign success.

```python
# Simulated conversion rate data
campaign_dates = pd.date_range('2023-01-01',
periods=12, freq='M')
visitors = np.random.randint(1000, 5000, 12)
conversions = np.random.randint(100, 1000, 12)

conversion_rate = conversions / visitors * 100

df_campaign = pd.DataFrame({
    'Date': campaign_dates,
    'Visitors': visitors,
    'Conversions': conversions,
    'Conversion Rate (%)': conversion_rate
})

# Create line plot for conversion rate
fig = px.line(df_campaign, x='Date',
y='Conversion Rate (%)', title="Campaign
Conversion Rate Over Time")
fig.show()
```

◆ **Explanation**:

- `conversion_rate = conversions / visitors * 100`: Calculates the **conversion rate** as a percentage.
- `px.line()`: Creates an interactive line chart to track conversion rates over time.

17.2.2 Visualizing ROI (Return on Investment)

ROI is a key metric for assessing the effectiveness of a campaign. It compares the return (profits) to the investment (costs), helping to evaluate whether the campaign was worth the expenditure.

python

```python
# Simulate campaign ROI data
campaign_spend = np.random.randint(500, 2000, 12)
revenue = campaign_spend * np.random.uniform(3, 5, 12)  # Assume revenue is 3-5 times spend

roi = (revenue - campaign_spend) / campaign_spend * 100  # ROI formula

df_roi = pd.DataFrame({
    'Date': campaign_dates,
    'Campaign Spend': campaign_spend,
    'Revenue': revenue,
    'ROI (%)': roi
```

```
})

# Plotting the ROI
fig = px.bar(df_roi, x='Date', y='ROI (%)',
title="ROI for Marketing Campaigns")
fig.show()
```

◆ **Explanation**:

- The **ROI** is calculated by subtracting the **campaign spend** from **revenue**, then dividing by the **spend**.
- `px.bar()`: Creates a **bar chart** to show ROI over time for each campaign.

17.3 Visualizing A/B Test Results and Customer Acquisition Cost

A/B testing is a key method for optimizing marketing strategies. By testing two versions of a campaign or webpage, businesses can determine which version yields better results. Another critical metric is **Customer Acquisition Cost (CAC)**, which measures the cost of acquiring a customer.

17.3.1 Visualizing A/B Test Results

A/B tests compare two variations to measure performance. A common A/B test in marketing is testing different landing page designs.

python

```
# Simulated A/B Test data
test_dates     =     pd.date_range('2023-01-01',
periods=10, freq='D')
version_A_conversions   =   np.random.randint(50,
150, 10)
version_B_conversions   =   np.random.randint(60,
160, 10)

df_ab_test = pd.DataFrame({
    'Date': test_dates,
    'Version         A         Conversions':
version_A_conversions,
    'Version         B         Conversions':
version_B_conversions
})

# Line plot for A/B test conversion comparison
fig = px.line(df_ab_test, x='Date', y=['Version
A Conversions', 'Version B Conversions'],
            title="A/B      Test      Results:
Conversion Comparison")
```

211

```
fig.show()
```

♦ Explanation:

- The **A/B test** data is visualized with a **line chart**, comparing conversions for **Version A** and **Version B**.
- This allows businesses to identify which version performed better over time.

17.3.2 Visualizing Customer Acquisition Cost (CAC)

Customer Acquisition Cost (CAC) is a critical metric that indicates how much it costs to acquire a single customer. It's essential for evaluating the efficiency of marketing campaigns.

python

```python
# Simulated CAC data
cost_per_acquisition  =  np.random.randint(30,
200, 12)  # Cost to acquire one customer
new_customers = np.random.randint(10, 100, 12)

cac = cost_per_acquisition * new_customers

df_cac = pd.DataFrame({
    'Month':        pd.date_range('2023-01-01',
periods=12, freq='M'),
```

```
    'CAC': cac
})

# Plot CAC over time
fig = px.line(df_cac, x='Month', y='CAC',
title="Customer Acquisition Cost (CAC) Over
Time")
fig.show()
```

✦ **Explanation**:

- The **Customer Acquisition Cost** (CAC) is calculated by multiplying **cost per acquisition** by the number of **new customers**.
- A **line chart** helps visualize how CAC changes over time, helping businesses optimize their marketing budgets.

17.4 Summary and Next Steps

In this chapter, we:

- Created **sales performance dashboards** to track key sales metrics.
- Visualized **campaign performance** by creating **conversion rate** and **ROI** charts.

- Built visualizations for **A/B test results** and **Customer Acquisition Cost (CAC)** to help evaluate marketing strategy effectiveness.

Next Chapter: Advanced Marketing Analytics with Geospatial Data

In the next chapter, we will explore advanced marketing analytics by utilizing **geospatial data** to map customer locations, analyze market penetration, and visualize regional performance across different campaigns.

◆ **Key Takeaway**: **Sales and marketing data visualizations**, including **conversion rates**, **ROI**, and **A/B test results**, are essential tools for measuring campaign effectiveness and optimizing strategies. **Plotly** and **Dash** provide powerful, interactive visualizations that help decision-makers gain actionable insights for business growth. 🚀

CHAPTER 19

Visualizing Survey Data

17.1 Visualizing Likert Scale Data and Survey Responses

Surveys are a vital tool for gathering feedback from customers, employees, or the general public. One common type of survey data is **Likert scale data**, which measures attitudes or opinions on a scale (e.g., 1 to 5, with 1 being "Strongly Disagree" and 5 being "Strongly Agree"). Visualizing this type of data allows businesses to understand patterns and sentiment across different respondents.

17.1.1 Likert Scale Data Visualization

Likert scale responses can be visualized using **bar charts** or **stacked bar charts**, which show the distribution of answers for each survey question. This type of visualization makes it easier to see how respondents feel about a given topic or statement.

Here's an example of visualizing Likert scale data using **Plotly** for an interactive, dynamic bar chart:

```python
python

import plotly.express as px
import pandas as pd

# Example survey data: Likert scale responses (1-5)
data = {
    'Question': ['Service Quality', 'Product Satisfaction', 'Customer Support', 'Value for Money'],
    'Strongly Disagree': [10, 5, 2, 4],
    'Disagree': [15, 7, 5, 8],
    'Neutral': [25, 15, 12, 14],
    'Agree': [30, 40, 35, 50],
    'Strongly Agree': [20, 30, 40, 24]
}

df = pd.DataFrame(data)

# Create a stacked bar chart to visualize Likert scale data
fig = px.bar(df, x='Question', y=['Strongly Disagree', 'Disagree', 'Neutral', 'Agree', 'Strongly Agree'],
             title="Survey Responses on Likert Scale",
             labels={'value': 'Number of Responses', 'Question': 'Survey Question'},
```

```
height=400)
```

```
fig.show()
```

♦ **Explanation**:

- `px.bar()`: Creates a **stacked bar chart** where the height of each bar represents the number of responses for each Likert scale level.
- The stacked nature of the bar allows users to easily compare the responses across different categories (Strongly Disagree to Strongly Agree).

17.1.2 Customizing Likert Scale Charts

You can also customize these charts to improve readability and highlight specific trends, such as **adding annotations**, changing **colors**, or introducing **interactive filters**:

```
python
```

```
fig.update_traces(texttemplate='%{y}',
textposition='inside', insidetextanchor='start')
fig.update_layout(barmode='stack', title="Survey
Responses by Question", xaxis_title="Questions",
yaxis_title="Responses")
fig.show()
```

◆ **Explanation**:

- `texttemplate='%{y}'`: Displays the count of responses inside the bars.
- `barmode='stack'`: Ensures the bars are stacked to show the total number of responses across all categories.

17.2 Creating Survey Dashboards and Insights

A survey dashboard is a powerful way to present multiple metrics from a survey in a single, interactive interface. It helps businesses gain **insights** and track performance over time.

17.2.1 Building a Survey Dashboard with Dash

In this example, we'll create a simple **survey dashboard** that includes key metrics such as **average ratings**, **distribution of Likert scale responses**, and **response count by category**.

python

```
import dash
from dash import dcc, html
import plotly.express as px
import pandas as pd
```

218

```python
import numpy as np

# Example survey data
df = pd.DataFrame({
    'Question': ['Service Quality', 'Product
Satisfaction', 'Customer Support', 'Value for
Money'],
    'Strongly Disagree': [10, 5, 2, 4],
    'Disagree': [15, 7, 5, 8],
    'Neutral': [25, 15, 12, 14],
    'Agree': [30, 40, 35, 50],
    'Strongly Agree': [20, 30, 40, 24]
})

# Create a bar chart for Likert scale responses
bar_fig = px.bar(df, x='Question', y=['Strongly
Disagree', 'Disagree', 'Neutral', 'Agree',
'Strongly Agree'],
                 title="Survey Responses on
Likert Scale")

# Create a pie chart for overall sentiment (based
on the sum of ratings)
sentiment_data = {
    'Sentiment': ['Positive', 'Neutral',
'Negative'],
    'Responses': [df['Agree'].sum() +
df['Strongly Agree'].sum(), df['Neutral'].sum(),
```

```
            df['Disagree'].sum()           +
df['Strongly Disagree'].sum()]
}


df_sentiment = pd.DataFrame(sentiment_data)
pie_fig          =           px.pie(df_sentiment,
names='Sentiment',            values='Responses',
title="Overall Sentiment")

# Initialize Dash app
app = dash.Dash(__name__)

app.layout = html.Div([
    html.H1("Survey Dashboard"),
    dcc.Graph(id='likert-bar', figure=bar_fig),
    dcc.Graph(id='sentiment-pie',
figure=pie_fig),
])

if __name__ == '__main__':
    app.run_server(debug=True)
```

◆ Explanation:

- This example uses **Dash** to create an interactive dashboard with a **bar chart** for Likert scale data and a **pie chart** to show overall sentiment.
- `dcc.Graph()`: Displays the respective charts, allowing users to interact with them (e.g., zooming, panning).

17.2.2 Customizing Dashboards for Business Needs

Dashboards can be further customized by adding additional **interactivity** (e.g., dropdown filters to display responses by demographics or date ranges) or including **performance benchmarks** to provide context for the survey results.

17.3 Visualizing Open-Ended Responses Using Word Clouds

Open-ended survey questions provide rich qualitative data, but they can be challenging to analyze. **Word clouds** are a popular way to visualize the frequency of words in a collection of text, making it easier to identify key themes, topics, or sentiments.

17.3.1 Creating Word Clouds from Survey Responses

Here's how to generate a **word cloud** from open-ended responses in a survey:

python

```
from wordcloud import WordCloud
import matplotlib.pyplot as plt
```

```python
# Example survey open-ended responses
responses = [
    "Great service, will buy again.",
    "Product quality is poor, but support was
helpful.",
    "Amazing experience, will recommend to
friends.",
    "Service was slow and the product did not
meet expectations.",
    "Happy with the product, customer service was
excellent."
]

# Combine all responses into a single string
text = " ".join(responses)

# Generate the word cloud
wordcloud = WordCloud(width=800, height=400,
background_color='white').generate(text)

# Plot the word cloud
plt.figure(figsize=(10, 6))
plt.imshow(wordcloud, interpolation='bilinear')
plt.axis('off')  # Hide axis
plt.title("Word Cloud for Open-Ended Responses")
plt.show()
```

♦ **Explanation**:

- The **WordCloud** library generates a **word cloud** where the size of each word corresponds to its frequency in the dataset.

- **plt.imshow()** renders the word cloud image, and **plt.axis('off')** hides the axis to focus purely on the visualization.

17.3.2 Customizing Word Clouds

You can customize the word cloud to highlight specific themes or exclude common words (e.g., "the", "and", "is") using **stopwords** or adjusting colors.

python

```
# Adding stopwords and customizing word cloud
colors
stopwords = set(["will", "to", "the", "is",
"and", "of"])

wordcloud = WordCloud(width=800, height=400,
background_color='white', stopwords=stopwords,

colormap='Blues').generate(text)

# Plot with customization
plt.figure(figsize=(10, 6))
plt.imshow(wordcloud, interpolation='bilinear')
```

223

```
plt.axis('off')
plt.title("Customized Word Cloud for Open-Ended
Responses")
plt.show()
```

✦ Explanation:

- **stopwords**: Prevents common words from appearing in the word cloud.
- **colormap='Blues'**: Customizes the color palette of the word cloud to use shades of blue.

17.4 Summary and Next Steps

In this chapter, we:

- **Visualized Likert scale data** using bar charts and stacked bar charts to track responses to survey questions.
- **Created a survey dashboard** combining multiple visualizations (e.g., Likert scale responses and overall sentiment) to provide comprehensive insights.
- Generated **word clouds** from open-ended survey responses to identify key themes and sentiments.

Next Chapter: Advanced Survey Analytics

In the next chapter, we will delve into **advanced survey analytics**, including **sentiment analysis, text mining**, and **topic modeling**, to extract deeper insights from open-ended responses and enhance decision-making.

◆ **Key Takeaway**: Survey data visualizations, including **Likert scale responses, sentiment analysis**, and **word clouds**, help businesses gain actionable insights from quantitative and qualitative feedback. These visualizations allow stakeholders to understand customer perceptions and make informed decisions. 🚀

CHAPTER 20

Interactive Business Dashboards with Plotly

17.1 Creating Interactive Business Dashboards

Interactive business dashboards allow businesses to track real-time performance and make data-driven decisions quickly. By presenting key metrics and KPIs in a centralized, interactive format, dashboards make it easier for users to engage with the data, filter results, and explore insights.

In this chapter, we'll learn how to use **Plotly Dash** to create an interactive dashboard that displays business data, such as sales performance, revenue, and customer insights. Dashboards like these enable users to interact with the data, providing a deeper understanding of business performance.

17.1.1 Building a Basic Interactive Dashboard with Dash

The **Dash** library in Python is a great tool for building **interactive dashboards**. It enables us to integrate interactive charts, sliders, and drop-down menus into a web interface. Below is an example of creating a dashboard that tracks **monthly sales** and allows users to filter data by **region**.

python

```python
import dash
from dash import dcc, html
import plotly.express as px
import pandas as pd
import numpy as np

# Sample business data: Sales by region and month
np.random.seed(0)
regions = ['North', 'South', 'East', 'West']
months = pd.date_range('2023-01-01', periods=12,
freq='M')

data = {
    'Date': np.tile(months, 4),
    'Region': np.repeat(regions, 12),
    'Sales': np.random.randint(1000, 5000, 48)
}

df = pd.DataFrame(data)

# Create a Dash app
app = dash.Dash(__name__)

app.layout = html.Div([
```

```python
    html.H1("Interactive Business Dashboard"),

    # Dropdown menu to select region
    html.Label('Select Region:'),
    dcc.Dropdown(
        id='region-dropdown',
        options=[{'label':    region,    'value':
region} for region in regions],
        value='North',  # Default value
        style={'width': '50%'}
    ),

    # Line chart to display sales trend
    dcc.Graph(
        id='sales-trend',
    )
])

# Callback to update the sales chart based on
selected region
@app.callback(
    dash.dependencies.Output('sales-trend',
'figure'),
    [dash.dependencies.Input('region-dropdown',
'value')]
)
def update_sales_trend(selected_region):
    filtered_df    =    df[df['Region']    ==
selected_region]
```

228

```
    fig    =     px.line(filtered_df,    x='Date',
y='Sales',        title=f"Sales        Trend        for
{selected_region} Region")
    return fig


if __name__ == '__main__':
    app.run_server(debug=True)
```

◆ **Explanation**:

- `dcc.Dropdown()`: Adds a **dropdown menu** that allows users to select a region.
- `dcc.Graph()`: Displays the **sales trend** chart.
- The `@app.callback()` function updates the chart based on the selected region.

17.2 Filtering and Drilling Down Data Using Drop-Down Menus and Sliders

Interactive dashboards become much more valuable when users can **filter** and **drill down** into specific aspects of the data. **Drop-down menus**, **sliders**, and other interactive components can be used to give users more control over the data they want to view.

229

17.2.1 Filtering Data with Drop-Down Menus

Drop-down menus allow users to filter the data by specific categories or dimensions. For example, you can add a drop-down to filter data by **product category**, **sales representative**, or any other business variable.

python

```python
# Dropdown menu for filtering by product category
product_categories        =        ['Electronics',
'Furniture', 'Clothing']

app.layout = html.Div([
    html.H1("Interactive Sales Dashboard"),

    html.Label('Select Product Category:'),
    dcc.Dropdown(
        id='product-dropdown',
        options=[{'label': category, 'value':
category} for category in product_categories],
        value='Electronics',  # Default value
        style={'width': '50%'}
    ),

    dcc.Graph(id='sales-product')
])
```

```
# Callback to update the graph based on selected
product category
@app.callback(
    dash.dependencies.Output('sales-product',
'figure'),
    [dash.dependencies.Input('product-
dropdown', 'value')]
)
def update_product_sales(selected_product):
    filtered_data    =    df[df['Region']    ==
selected_product]  # Simulating product filtering
    fig    =    px.bar(filtered_data,    x='Date',
y='Sales',           title=f"Sales           for
{selected_product}")
    return fig
```

◆ **Explanation**:

- `dcc.Dropdown()`: Filters the data based on the **product category**.
- The callback updates the chart when the product category is changed.

17.2.2 Drilling Down Data Using Sliders

Sliders are another interactive component that enables users to **drill down** into data by adjusting a specific parameter, such as a **time range** or **numerical value**.

231

```python
python

# Create a slider to adjust the number of sales
shown
app.layout = html.Div([
    html.H1("Sales Over Time Dashboard"),

    html.Label('Select Sales Threshold:'),
    dcc.Slider(
        id='sales-slider',
        min=1000,
        max=5000,
        step=500,
        value=3000,  # Default value
        marks={i: f'{i}' for i in range(1000,
5001, 1000)}
    ),

    dcc.Graph(id='filtered-sales')
])

# Callback to update the sales chart based on
slider input
@app.callback(
    dash.dependencies.Output('filtered-sales',
'figure'),
    [dash.dependencies.Input('sales-slider',
'value')]
)
```

```
def update_sales_threshold(sales_threshold):
    filtered_sales    =    df[df['Sales']    >=
sales_threshold]
    fig   =   px.bar(filtered_sales,   x='Date',
y='Sales',          title=f"Sales          above
{sales_threshold}")
    return fig
```

◆ **Explanation**:

- `dcc.Slider()`: Allows the user to adjust the **sales threshold**.
- The chart updates dynamically to show only sales that exceed the selected threshold.

17.3 Displaying Actionable Insights from Interactive Dashboards

Dashboards should not only display data; they should also provide **actionable insights** to guide decision-making. In this section, we'll discuss how to integrate **summary statistics**, **KPIs**, and **real-time alerts** into your dashboard.

17.3.1 Displaying Summary Statistics

You can include **key metrics** such as the **average sales, highest performing regions**, or **overall revenue** in your dashboard to provide context to the visualized data.

python

```
# Calculate and display summary statistics
average_sales = df['Sales'].mean()

app.layout = html.Div([
    html.H1("Business Insights Dashboard"),
    html.Div(f"Average                Sales:
${average_sales:.2f}"),
    dcc.Graph(id='sales-performance')
])

# Further analysis or visualizations go here
```

◆ **Explanation**:

- `df['Sales'].mean()`: Calculates the **average sales** to display as an insight.
- This summary statistic can guide decision-makers on overall sales performance.

17.3.2 Real-Time Alerts and Notifications

Integrating **real-time alerts** based on specific criteria, such as **sales targets** or **performance anomalies**, allows users to stay updated on important metrics.

python

```python
# Check if sales exceed a certain threshold and
display a notification
if df['Sales'].sum() > 50000:
    alert_message = "Sales target exceeded! Keep
up the good work!"
else:
    alert_message  =  "Sales  target  not  yet
reached."

app.layout = html.Div([
    html.H1("Sales Dashboard"),
    html.Div(alert_message,      style={'color':
'red', 'font-weight': 'bold'}),
    dcc.Graph(id='sales-trend')
])
```

◆ **Explanation**:

- This approach **alerts** users when **sales exceed a target** by displaying a **real-time message**.

- Such alerts are valuable for driving action or providing motivation in a business environment.

17.4 Summary and Next Steps

In this chapter, we:

- Built an **interactive dashboard** using **Plotly Dash** to track key sales metrics.
- Integrated **interactive filters** using **drop-down menus** and **sliders** to allow users to explore different segments of the data.
- Provided **actionable insights** through summary statistics, real-time alerts, and customizable visualizations.

Next Chapter: Advanced Data Visualization Techniques for Business Analytics

In the next chapter, we will explore **advanced data visualization techniques** such as **heatmaps**, **funnel visualizations**, and **interactive forecasting**, enabling deeper insights into business performance.

236

✦ **Key Takeaway**: **Interactive dashboards** empower decision-makers by providing them with real-time, **dynamic visualizations** and **actionable insights**. Using **Plotly Dash**, you can create **user-friendly** dashboards that allow users to filter and drill down data for deeper business analysis. 🚀

PART 5

REAL-WORLD APPLICATIONS

CHAPTER 21

Visualizing Healthcare Data

21.1 Visualizing Patient Health Metrics, Medical Records, and Treatment Outcomes

The healthcare industry generates vast amounts of data, and visualizing this data effectively is essential for improving patient care, streamlining treatment, and driving informed decisions. By visualizing **patient health metrics**, **medical records**, and **treatment outcomes**, healthcare professionals can gain insights into individual and population health, identify trends, and evaluate the effectiveness of treatments.

21.1.1 Visualizing Patient Health Metrics

Health metrics such as **blood pressure**, **heart rate**, **cholesterol levels**, and **BMI (Body Mass Index)** are key indicators of a patient's well-being. Plotting these metrics over time helps doctors assess trends and make proactive treatment decisions.

Here's an example of visualizing health metrics using **Plotly** to create a **line chart** for monitoring **blood pressure** and **heart rate**:

python

```python
import plotly.graph_objects as go
import pandas as pd
import numpy as np

# Sample patient health data (Date, Blood
Pressure, Heart Rate)
dates = pd.date_range('2023-01-01', periods=12,
freq='M')
blood_pressure = np.random.randint(110, 140, 12)
heart_rate = np.random.randint(60, 90, 12)

# Create a DataFrame
df_health = pd.DataFrame({
    'Date': dates,
    'Blood Pressure': blood_pressure,
    'Heart Rate': heart_rate
})

# Create line charts for health metrics
fig = go.Figure()
```

```
fig.add_trace(go.Scatter(x=df_health['Date'],
y=df_health['Blood    Pressure'],    mode='lines',
name='Blood Pressure'))
fig.add_trace(go.Scatter(x=df_health['Date'],
y=df_health['Heart    Rate'],    mode='lines',
name='Heart Rate'))


fig.update_layout(
    title="Patient Health Metrics Over Time",
    xaxis_title="Date",
    yaxis_title="Metric Value",
    legend_title="Health Metrics"
)


fig.show()
```

◈ Explanation:

- **go.Scatter()**: Creates a **line chart** that tracks the **blood pressure** and **heart rate** for a patient over time.
- The line chart allows healthcare professionals to monitor trends in key metrics and evaluate any potential health risks.

21.1.2 Visualizing Medical Records and Treatment Outcomes

Visualizing medical records and the effectiveness of **treatment plans** allows doctors to track patient progress, identify the success of treatments, and make data-driven decisions. For instance, **treatment effectiveness** can be visualized by comparing **pre-treatment** and **post-treatment** metrics.

python

```python
# Simulated pre-treatment and post-treatment data
treatment_outcomes = pd.DataFrame({
    'Patient ID': [1, 2, 3, 4, 5],
    'Pre-Treatment BP': [130, 135, 140, 125, 145],
    'Post-Treatment BP': [120, 130, 125, 118, 138]
})

# Create a bar chart to visualize treatment outcomes
import plotly.express as px
fig = px.bar(treatment_outcomes, x='Patient ID',
y=['Pre-Treatment BP', 'Post-Treatment BP'],
            title="Pre-Treatment vs Post-Treatment Blood Pressure",
            labels={'Patient ID': 'Patient ID', 'value': 'Blood Pressure'},
            barmode='group')

fig.show()
```

◆ **Explanation**:

- The **bar chart** compares **pre-treatment** and **post-treatment** blood pressure values, showing the effectiveness of the treatment plan.
- **Group bar charts** are ideal for comparing data across multiple categories (in this case, patients).

21.2 Creating Visualizations for Disease Spread and Treatment Effectiveness

In the context of public health, visualizing the **spread of disease** and evaluating the **effectiveness of treatment** can help authorities make informed decisions. Disease spread data, often collected over time, can be visualized using **heatmaps**, **line charts**, or **choropleth maps**.

21.2.1 Visualizing Disease Spread with Heatmaps

Heatmaps are powerful for visualizing **geospatial** data and can help track the **spread of disease** in different regions. Below is an example using a **heatmap** to visualize disease incidents across different regions.

python

```python
import plotly.express as px

# Example disease spread data by region
regions = ['North', 'South', 'East', 'West']
disease_cases = [150, 200, 350, 100]

# Create a heatmap of disease cases
df_disease = pd.DataFrame({
    'Region': regions,
    'Disease Cases': disease_cases
})

fig = px.bar(df_disease, x='Region', y='Disease
Cases',
            title="Disease Spread by Region",
color='Disease Cases',
            color_continuous_scale='Viridis')

fig.show()
```

◆ Explanation:

- The **heatmap** uses color intensity to represent the **number of disease cases** in different regions.
- Color gradients, such as **Viridis**, help highlight regions with higher disease incidents.

244

21.2.2 Visualizing Treatment Effectiveness Across Regions

Treatment effectiveness can be visualized through **comparison charts** that show how regions or different patient groups respond to treatment. By plotting the **recovery rate** or **percentage improvement**, healthcare professionals can better allocate resources.

python

```
# Simulated treatment effectiveness data
regions = ['North', 'South', 'East', 'West']
recovery_rate = [85, 90, 80, 95]  # Recovery rate
in percentage

# Create bar chart for treatment effectiveness by
region
fig     =     px.bar(df_disease,     x='Region',
y=recovery_rate,
          title="Treatment  Effectiveness  by
Region",
          labels={'Region':        'Region',
'value': 'Recovery Rate (%)'})

fig.show()
```

◆ **Explanation**:

- The **bar chart** compares **treatment effectiveness** (recovery rates) across regions, helping to identify where treatments are most successful.

21.3 Using Dash for Real-Time Healthcare Data Visualization

For real-time monitoring and visualization of healthcare data, **Dash** can be used to build dynamic, interactive applications that update in real-time. These dashboards can be used for monitoring patient health, tracking **emergency department** performance, or even visualizing the status of **ICU beds**.

21.3.1 Building a Real-Time Healthcare Dashboard with Dash

In this section, we'll create a **real-time healthcare dashboard** that updates a hospital's **patient admission data** and **bed occupancy**.

python

```
import dash
from dash import dcc, html
import plotly.express as px
```

```python
import pandas as pd
import numpy as np

# Simulate real-time data (patient admission and
bed occupancy)
time_intervals   =   pd.date_range('2023-01-01',
periods=100, freq='H')
patients_admitted   =   np.random.randint(5,   20,
100)
bed_occupancy = np.random.randint(50, 100, 100)

df_real_time = pd.DataFrame({
    'Time': time_intervals,
    'Patients Admitted': patients_admitted,
    'Bed Occupancy (%)': bed_occupancy
})

# Create Dash app
app = dash.Dash(__name__)

app.layout = html.Div([
    html.H1("Real-Time Healthcare Dashboard"),

    # Graph to show patient admission
    dcc.Graph(
        id='patients-admitted',
        figure=px.line(df_real_time,   x='Time',
y='Patients Admitted', title="Patients Admitted
Over Time")
```

```
    ),

    # Graph to show bed occupancy rate
    dcc.Graph(
        id='bed-occupancy',
        figure=px.line(df_real_time,   x='Time',
y='Bed Occupancy (%)', title="Bed Occupancy Over
Time")
    ),
])

if __name__ == '__main__':
    app.run_server(debug=True)
```

♦ Explanation:

- **Dash**: This app uses **Dash** to create a **real-time dashboard** for monitoring **patient admissions** and **bed occupancy** in a hospital.
- `px.line()`: This function is used to create **line charts** that show trends in data over time (in this case, admissions and bed occupancy).

21.4 Summary and Next Steps

In this chapter, we:

248

- Visualized **patient health metrics**, including **blood pressure** and **heart rate**, to track patient progress and make treatment decisions.
- Created visualizations to monitor **disease spread** and evaluate **treatment effectiveness** across different regions.
- Built a **real-time healthcare dashboard** using **Dash** to track critical data such as **patient admissions** and **bed occupancy**.

Next Chapter: Advanced Healthcare Data Analytics

In the next chapter, we will explore **advanced analytics** for healthcare data, including **predictive modeling**, **disease forecasting**, and **machine learning applications** to enhance patient care and operational efficiency.

◆ **Key Takeaway**: Visualizing healthcare data, such as **patient health metrics**, **disease spread**, and **treatment outcomes**, enables healthcare professionals to make informed decisions and improve patient care. Tools like **Plotly** and **Dash** provide powerful ways to create real-time, interactive visualizations for dynamic healthcare environments. 🚀

CHAPTER 22

Exploring Social Media Data

22.1 Visualizing Social Media Engagement Metrics

Social media engagement is a critical indicator of how well content is resonating with an audience. Engagement metrics, such as **likes**, **shares**, **comments**, and **click-through rates (CTR)**, help businesses, brands, and influencers gauge their audience's level of interest and interaction with their posts.

By visualizing these metrics, organizations can quickly assess their social media performance, optimize their content strategies, and drive more targeted marketing efforts.

22.1.1 Visualizing Engagement Metrics Over Time

To track engagement over time, you can use **line charts** or **bar charts**. These charts help show the trend of engagement levels, making it easier to identify peaks (successful campaigns or posts) and dips (when engagement is low).

251

Here's an example of visualizing **likes**, **comments**, and **shares** over time:

python

```
import plotly.express as px
import pandas as pd
import numpy as np

# Simulated social media engagement data over 12
days
dates = pd.date_range('2023-01-01', periods=12,
freq='D')
likes = np.random.randint(100, 1000, 12)
comments = np.random.randint(10, 300, 12)
shares = np.random.randint(5, 150, 12)

df_engagement = pd.DataFrame({
    'Date': dates,
    'Likes': likes,
    'Comments': comments,
    'Shares': shares
})

# Create a line chart for engagement metrics
fig    =    px.line(df_engagement,    x='Date',
y=['Likes', 'Comments', 'Shares'],
            title="Social   Media   Engagement
Over Time",
```

```
            labels={'value':          'Engagement
Count', 'Date': 'Date'})
fig.show()
```

◆ Explanation:

- **px.line()**: This creates a **line chart** that displays engagement metrics over time. It shows **likes, comments**, and **shares**, allowing you to track how engagement varies from day to day.

- **y=['Likes', 'Comments', 'Shares']**: Plots multiple metrics in a single chart for easy comparison.

22.1.2 Creating Bar Charts for Engagement Comparison

To compare engagement levels across multiple social media platforms (e.g., **Instagram, Twitter, Facebook**), **bar charts** can be used. These charts help compare engagement performance across platforms at a glance.

python

```
# Simulate engagement metrics for three platforms
platforms = ['Instagram', 'Twitter', 'Facebook']
likes_platform = [1200, 800, 950]
comments_platform = [300, 220, 275]
shares_platform = [150, 120, 200]
```

```
df_platform_engagement = pd.DataFrame({
    'Platform': platforms,
    'Likes': likes_platform,
    'Comments': comments_platform,
    'Shares': shares_platform
})


# Create a grouped bar chart to compare
engagement across platforms
fig        =        px.bar(df_platform_engagement,
x='Platform', y=['Likes', 'Comments', 'Shares'],
            title="Social    Media    Engagement
Comparison by Platform",
            barmode='group',    labels={'value':
'Engagement  Count',  'Platform':  'Social  Media
Platform'})
fig.show()
```

◆ **Explanation**:

- The **grouped bar chart** compares engagement metrics across different social media platforms.
- `barmode='group'`: This option groups the bars for each platform, making it easy to compare metrics like **likes**, **comments**, and **shares** side by side.

22.2 Creating Sentiment Analysis Dashboards

Sentiment analysis helps businesses understand how people feel about a brand, product, or service based on social media interactions. By analyzing **positive**, **negative**, and **neutral** sentiments in posts or comments, businesses can better tailor their marketing strategies and responses.

22.2.1 Visualizing Sentiment Analysis with Plotly

You can use **bar charts**, **pie charts**, or **word clouds** to represent sentiment analysis results. Here's how to create a simple **pie chart** to show the distribution of **positive**, **negative**, and **neutral** sentiments in social media comments.

python

```python
import plotly.graph_objects as go

# Simulated sentiment analysis data
sentiment = ['Positive', 'Neutral', 'Negative']
sentiment_counts = [450, 300, 150]

# Create a pie chart for sentiment distribution
fig    =    go.Figure(go.Pie(labels=sentiment,
values=sentiment_counts,         title="Sentiment
Analysis of Social Media Posts"))
fig.show()
```

◆ **Explanation**:

255

- **go.Pie()**: Creates a **pie chart** to visualize the sentiment distribution (positive, neutral, negative).
- **labels** and **values**: These specify the sentiment categories and their corresponding counts, respectively.

22.2.2 Sentiment Over Time

To track how sentiment changes over time (e.g., before and after a product launch), you can use a **line chart** or **stacked area chart**. This provides insight into how **public perception** evolves.

python

```
# Simulate sentiment over time (12 days)
dates = pd.date_range('2023-01-01', periods=12,
freq='D')
positive_sentiment = np.random.randint(100, 500,
12)
negative_sentiment = np.random.randint(50, 250,
12)
neutral_sentiment = np.random.randint(200, 500,
12)

df_sentiment_time = pd.DataFrame({
    'Date': dates,
    'Positive': positive_sentiment,
    'Negative': negative_sentiment,
```

```
    'Neutral': neutral_sentiment
})


# Create a stacked area chart for sentiment over
time
fig   =   px.area(df_sentiment_time,   x='Date',
y=['Positive', 'Negative', 'Neutral'],
          title="Sentiment Distribution Over
Time",
          labels={'value':        'Sentiment
Count', 'Date': 'Date'})
fig.show()
```

◆ **Explanation**:

- **px.area()**: Creates a **stacked area chart** that shows how **positive**, **negative**, and **neutral** sentiments change over time.
- This is valuable for identifying trends in social media conversations.

22.3 Mapping Social Media Data Using Geospatial Visualizations

Geospatial visualizations help businesses understand the **geographic distribution** of social media activity. By

257

mapping posts, hashtags, or mentions, companies can analyze the geographic spread of social media engagement, enabling location-based marketing strategies.

22.3.1 Mapping Social Media Activity on a World Map

You can use **Plotly's choropleth maps** or **scatter geo maps** to visualize the geographic spread of social media activity. For example, here's how to plot social media mentions across countries.

```python
import plotly.express as px

# Simulated social media activity by country
countries = ['USA', 'Canada', 'UK', 'India',
'Australia']
mentions = [1200, 800, 500, 1500, 700]

# Create a DataFrame
df_geo = pd.DataFrame({
    'Country': countries,
    'Mentions': mentions
})

# Create a choropleth map to visualize social
media mentions by country
```

```
fig = px.choropleth(df_geo, locations='Country',
locationmode='country names',
                    color='Mentions',
hover_name='Country',
color_continuous_scale='Viridis',
                    title="Social Media Mentions
by Country")
fig.show()
```

◆ Explanation:

- **px.choropleth()**: Creates a **choropleth map** to visualize social media mentions by country.

- **color_continuous_scale='Viridis'**: Adds a color scale to visually distinguish countries with higher mentions from those with fewer.

22.3.2 Geospatial Visualization of Social Media Engagement

Another option for geospatial data visualization is **scatter geo maps**, which plot social media engagement data (e.g., likes, shares) based on location.

```
python
```

```
# Simulated geospatial data for social media
engagement
```

```
locations = ['New York', 'Los Angeles', 'London',
'Mumbai', 'Sydney']
latitudes = [40.7128, 34.0522, 51.5074, 19.0760,
-33.8688]
longitudes = [-74.0060, -118.2437, -0.1278,
72.8777, 151.2093]
engagement = [1500, 2000, 1200, 1800, 1300]

# Create a scatter geo map
fig = px.scatter_geo(df_geo, lat=latitudes,
lon=longitudes, size=engagement,
                    hover_name=locations,
title="Social Media Engagement by Location",
                    projection="natural earth")
fig.show()
```

◆ **Explanation**:

- **px.scatter_geo()**: Plots engagement data on a **geo map** using latitude and longitude values.
- The size of the markers represents **social media engagement**, such as the number of likes or shares.

22.4 Summary and Next Steps

In this chapter, we:

- Created visualizations for **social media engagement metrics**, such as likes, comments, and shares, using **line charts** and **bar charts**.

- Built **sentiment analysis** dashboards, displaying positive, neutral, and negative sentiment in social media interactions.

- Visualized the **geographic distribution** of social media activity with **choropleth maps** and **scatter geo maps** to gain insights into audience reach and location-based trends.

Next Chapter: Advanced Social Media Analytics with Machine Learning

In the next chapter, we will delve into **advanced social media analytics**, such as **predictive modeling**, **trend analysis**, and **network analysis** to uncover deeper insights from social media data.

◆ **Key Takeaway**: Visualizing **social media data** through engagement metrics, sentiment analysis, and geospatial visualizations allows businesses to make informed decisions, optimize their marketing strategies, and improve customer engagement. Tools like **Plotly** provide interactive and insightful visualizations for exploring social media trends. 🚀

CHAPTER 23

Data Visualization for Sports Analytics

22.1 Visualizing Sports Performance Metrics

In sports analytics, performance metrics provide insights into an athlete's strengths, weaknesses, and overall game performance. Metrics such as **points scored**, **assists**, **rebounds**, **shot accuracy**, and **running speed** help coaches, analysts, and fans evaluate player contributions, improve training, and predict future performance.

22.1.1 Creating Line Charts for Performance Trends

To visualize the performance of a player over time, **line charts** are often used. They help track key metrics such as goals, assists, or points scored per game. For example, let's visualize the **points scored** by a basketball player over a season:

```python
import plotly.graph_objects as go
```

263

```python
import pandas as pd
import numpy as np

# Simulate points scored over a 10-game season
games = [f"Game {i}" for i in range(1, 11)]
points_scored = np.random.randint(10, 40, 10)   #
Points scored in each game

# Create a DataFrame
df_performance = pd.DataFrame({
    'Game': games,
    'Points Scored': points_scored
})

# Create a line chart for performance trends
fig = go.Figure()

fig.add_trace(go.Scatter(x=df_performance['Game
'],      y=df_performance['Points      Scored'],
mode='lines+markers', name='Points Scored'))

fig.update_layout(
    title="Player   Performance:   Points   Scored
Over 10 Games",
    xaxis_title="Game",
    yaxis_title="Points Scored",
)

fig.show()
```

✦ **Explanation**:

- `go.Figure()` and `go.Scatter()`: Creates a **line chart** to track **points scored** over a series of games.
- `mode='lines+markers'`: Plots the data with both **lines** and **markers** to visualize trends and specific data points.

22.1.2 Visualizing Shot Accuracy with a Bar Chart

For sports like basketball or soccer, **shot accuracy** is an important performance metric. We can visualize the player's **field goal percentage** or **shots made** over the course of a season using a **bar chart**.

python

```
import plotly.express as px

# Simulated shot data for a soccer player
shots_attempted = [12, 15, 13, 10, 9, 14, 16, 20,
17, 15]
shots_made = [8, 9, 7, 5, 6, 12, 14, 18, 15, 13]

df_shots = pd.DataFrame({
    'Game': games,
    'Shots Attempted': shots_attempted,
    'Shots Made': shots_made,
```

```
'Accuracy (%)': [round((made/attempted)*100,
2)  for  made,  attempted  in  zip(shots_made,
shots_attempted)]
})


# Create a bar chart for shot accuracy
fig  =  px.bar(df_shots,  x='Game',  y='Accuracy
(%)',
            title="Shot   Accuracy   Over   10
Games",
            labels={'Accuracy   (%)':   'Shot
Accuracy (%)'})

fig.show()
```

◆ Explanation:

- **px.bar()**: Creates a **bar chart** visualizing the **shot accuracy** (percentage of shots made).
- This chart allows you to track how accurately the player is performing over time.

22.2 Creating Player Comparison Charts and Performance Timelines

Comparing the performance of multiple players over time can help coaches and analysts make data-driven decisions. Visualization tools such as **scatter plots** or **radar charts** are great for comparing metrics like **goals scored**, **assists**, or **minutes played**.

22.2.1 Comparing Player Performance with Radar Charts

Radar charts are useful for comparing players across multiple performance metrics, such as **goals scored**, **assists**, **shots taken**, and **passes completed**.

```python
import plotly.express as px

# Simulated player performance data
players = ['Player A', 'Player B', 'Player C']
metrics = ['Goals', 'Assists', 'Shots', 'Passes
Completed']

# Data for each player
data = {
    'Player': ['Player A', 'Player B', 'Player
C'],
    'Goals': [25, 15, 30],
    'Assists': [10, 12, 15],
    'Shots': [150, 120, 140],
```

```
        'Passes Completed': [200, 180, 190]
}


df_players = pd.DataFrame(data)


# Create a radar chart for player comparison
fig          =           px.line_polar(df_players,
r=df_players.columns[1:],          theta=metrics,
line_close=True,
                    title="Player      Performance
Comparison",
                    color='Player',
markers=True)


fig.show()
```

◆ **Explanation**:

- **px.line_polar()**: Creates a **radar chart** to compare multiple players across different metrics.
- This chart allows easy comparison of how each player performs in various areas (e.g., **goals, assists, shots**).

22.2.2 Comparing Player Performance Over Time

For more detailed comparisons over time, a **line chart** with multiple players can visualize trends in metrics like **points**

scored or **goals made**. Here's an example comparing two players' performance:

```python
python

# Simulated performance data for two players over
time
player_a_points = np.random.randint(10, 30, 12)
player_b_points = np.random.randint(5, 25, 12)

df_comparison = pd.DataFrame({
    'Game': games,
    'Player A Points': player_a_points,
    'Player B Points': player_b_points
})

# Create a line chart for player performance
comparison
fig    =    px.line(df_comparison,    x='Game',
y=['Player A Points', 'Player B Points'],
            title="Player           Performance
Comparison Over Time",
            labels={'value': 'Points Scored',
'Game': 'Game'})

fig.show()
```

◆ **Explanation**:

- **`px.line()`**: Creates a **line chart** to compare how **Player A** and **Player B** perform over a series of games.
- This chart helps visualize trends, like whether one player consistently scores more points than the other.

22.3 Analyzing Match Data and Player Statistics Visually

Analyzing match data and player statistics is key to understanding team dynamics and individual player performance. **Heatmaps, scatter plots**, and **histograms** are useful for visualizing various aspects of match statistics, such as **shots taken, distance run**, or **pass completion rates**.

22.3.1 Visualizing Player Shot Placement with a Heatmap

A **heatmap** can be used to visualize the **placement of shots** on the field or court. This allows analysts to see where players are more likely to take shots, and where they might be most effective.

python

```
import plotly.graph_objects as go
```

```
# Simulated shot placement data (x, y coordinates
on the field)
x = np.random.randint(0, 100, 50)
y = np.random.randint(0, 100, 50)

# Create a heatmap for shot placement
fig    =    go.Figure(go.Histogram2d(x=x,    y=y,
colorscale='Viridis', nbinsx=10, nbinsy=10))

fig.update_layout(
    title="Player Shot Placement Heatmap",
    xaxis_title="Field X Position",
    yaxis_title="Field Y Position"
)

fig.show()
```

⬥ Explanation:

- **`go.Histogram2d()`**: This creates a **2D histogram**, which can be used as a **heatmap** to show where most shots are taken on the field (based on the **x** and **y** coordinates).

22.3.2 Analyzing Player Stats with Scatter Plots

To compare two or more player statistics, **scatter plots** are helpful in visualizing correlations between variables like **goals scored** versus **minutes played**.

python

```
# Simulated player stats (goals scored vs.
minutes played)
minutes_played = np.random.randint(10, 90, 12)
goals_scored = np.random.randint(0, 5, 12)

df_player_stats = pd.DataFrame({
    'Minutes Played': minutes_played,
    'Goals Scored': goals_scored
})

# Create a scatter plot for player performance
comparison
fig = px.scatter(df_player_stats, x='Minutes
Played', y='Goals Scored',
            title="Goals Scored vs. Minutes
Played",
            labels={'Minutes      Played':
'Minutes    Played', 'Goals   Scored':  'Goals
Scored'})

fig.show()
```

◈ Explanation:

- **px.scatter()**: This creates a **scatter plot** that visualizes the relationship between two variables— **minutes played** and **goals scored**. This can help identify patterns in how a player's time on the field affects their performance.

22.4 Summary and Next Steps

In this chapter, we:

- Visualized key **sports performance metrics** such as **points scored**, **shot accuracy**, and **goals** using various types of charts like **line charts**, **bar charts**, and **radar charts**.

- Compared player performance using **radar charts** and **line charts** to provide insights into player strengths and weaknesses.

- Analyzed match data and **player statistics** through **heatmaps** and **scatter plots** to reveal trends and correlations that help with decision-making.

Next Chapter: Advanced Sports Analytics with Predictive Modeling

In the next chapter, we will explore **advanced sports analytics** using **predictive modeling** to forecast player performance, team outcomes, and match results based on historical data.

◆ **Key Takeaway**: Visualizing **sports data**, such as **player performance**, **shot placement**, and **match statistics**, provides valuable insights that can help teams improve their strategy, understand player capabilities, and optimize overall performance. Visual tools like **Plotly** and **Dash** enable interactive and insightful analysis of this data. 🚀

CHAPTER 24

Visualizing IoT and Sensor Data

22.1 Working with Sensor Data for Real-Time Monitoring

The **Internet of Things (IoT)** is revolutionizing how we collect and analyze data from the physical world. IoT sensors are deployed in various applications, including **smart homes**, **wearable devices**, **industrial machines**, and **environmental monitoring**. These sensors generate massive amounts of real-time data, including **temperature**, **humidity**, **motion**, and **pressure** readings, which can be leveraged for real-time monitoring and decision-making.

Visualizing this data allows stakeholders to understand system performance, identify anomalies, and make data-driven decisions.

22.1.1 Sensor Data Collection and Processing

Typically, IoT data is collected by sensors and transmitted in real time to a cloud server or a local processing unit. The data can be visualized in several ways, depending on the context and type of sensor being used.

Let's simulate **temperature sensor data** collected over time for an IoT device and visualize it.

python

```python
import plotly.graph_objects as go
import pandas as pd
import numpy as np

# Simulate temperature data for an IoT sensor
over time
time = pd.date_range('2023-01-01', periods=50,
freq='H')
temperature = np.random.uniform(15, 30, 50)  #
Temperature in Celsius

df_sensor = pd.DataFrame({
    'Time': time,
    'Temperature (°C)': temperature
})

# Create a real-time temperature trend chart
fig = go.Figure()
```

```
fig.add_trace(go.Scatter(x=df_sensor['Time'],
y=df_sensor['Temperature                    (°C)'],
mode='lines+markers', name='Temperature'))

fig.update_layout(
    title="Real-Time Temperature Sensor Data",
    xaxis_title="Time",
    yaxis_title="Temperature (°C)",
)

fig.show()
```

◆ **Explanation**:

- **go.Scatter()**: Creates a **line chart** to visualize the temperature changes over time. This allows users to track the fluctuations in the data as the sensor continuously monitors the environment.

22.2 Visualizing IoT Data Streams with Dash

Dash by Plotly is an excellent tool for creating **interactive** and **real-time dashboards** to visualize IoT sensor data streams. Dashboards provide dynamic, user-friendly interfaces that allow users to monitor multiple devices or sensors in real time.

Let's create a **Dash app** that visualizes live IoT sensor data for **humidity** and **temperature**. The app will allow users to adjust the **time range** for the data being displayed.

22.2.1 Real-Time Monitoring of Sensor Data

python

```python
import dash
from dash import dcc, html
import plotly.graph_objects as go
import pandas as pd
import numpy as np


# Simulate real-time data stream for IoT sensors
(Temperature and Humidity)
time = pd.date_range('2023-01-01', periods=100,
freq='H')
temperature = np.random.uniform(15, 30, 100)
humidity = np.random.uniform(30, 70, 100)

df_iot_data = pd.DataFrame({
    'Time': time,
    'Temperature (°C)': temperature,
    'Humidity (%)': humidity
})

# Create Dash app
app = dash.Dash(__name__)
```

```python
app.layout = html.Div([
    html.H1("IoT Real-Time Data Dashboard"),

    # Temperature and Humidity Graph
    dcc.Graph(
        id='sensor-data-graph',
    ),

    html.Label('Select Time Range:'),
    dcc.Slider(
        id='time-slider',
        min=0,
        max=99,
        step=1,
        value=99,   # Default to the most recent
data
        marks={i: f'Hour {i+1}' for i in range(0,
100, 10)}
    ),
])

# Callback to update the graph based on selected
time range
@app.callback(
    dash.dependencies.Output('sensor-data-
graph', 'figure'),
    [dash.dependencies.Input('time-slider',
'value')]
)
```

```python
def update_graph(selected_hour):
    filtered_df                      =
df_iot_data.iloc[:selected_hour+1]   # Show data
up to the selected hour
    fig = go.Figure()

fig.add_trace(go.Scatter(x=filtered_df['Time'],
y=filtered_df['Temperature (°C)'], mode='lines',
name='Temperature (°C)'))

fig.add_trace(go.Scatter(x=filtered_df['Time'],
y=filtered_df['Humidity   (%)'],   mode='lines',
name='Humidity (%)'))

    fig.update_layout(
        title="IoT Sensor Data - Temperature &
Humidity Over Time",
        xaxis_title="Time",
        yaxis_title="Value",
    )

    return fig

if __name__ == '__main__':
    app.run_server(debug=True)
```

◆ **Explanation**:

280

- **Dash App**: The app features a **line graph** showing the **temperature** and **humidity** values over time. The **slider** allows the user to adjust the **time range** and view the data for the selected time period.

- `dcc.Slider()`: The **slider** provides an interactive way for users to filter and drill down into the data.

22.3 Building Dashboards for Device Performance and Health Monitoring

Monitoring the health and performance of devices, such as **IoT sensors** or **smart devices**, is essential for ensuring that systems are operating optimally. Visualizing metrics like **CPU usage**, **battery life**, and **error rates** allows businesses to proactively address potential issues before they escalate.

22.3.1 Visualizing Device Health Metrics

In this example, we'll simulate **device health data** such as **battery life** and **CPU usage** for IoT devices and visualize it in a **dashboard** that provides insights into device performance and health.

```python
```

```python
import dash
from dash import dcc, html
import plotly.graph_objects as go
import pandas as pd
import numpy as np


# Simulate IoT device health data (Battery and
CPU Usage)
devices = ['Device A', 'Device B', 'Device C',
'Device D']
battery = np.random.uniform(10, 100, 4)    #
Battery percentage
cpu_usage = np.random.uniform(30, 90, 4)  # CPU
Usage in percentage

df_device_health = pd.DataFrame({
    'Device': devices,
    'Battery (%)': battery,
    'CPU Usage (%)': cpu_usage
})


# Create Dash app
app = dash.Dash(__name__)

app.layout = html.Div([
    html.H1("IoT Device Health Dashboard"),

    # Bar chart for device battery status
    dcc.Graph(
```

```
        id='battery-status-graph',
    ),


    # Bar chart for device CPU usage
    dcc.Graph(
        id='cpu-usage-graph',
    ),
])


# Callback to update the device health charts
@app.callback(
    [dash.dependencies.Output('battery-status-
graph', 'figure'),
     dash.dependencies.Output('cpu-usage-
graph', 'figure')],
    []
)
def update_device_health():
    # Create battery health bar chart
    battery_fig                             =
go.Figure(go.Bar(x=df_device_health['Device'],
y=df_device_health['Battery (%)'], name='Battery
(%)'))
    battery_fig.update_layout(
        title="Device Battery Status",
        xaxis_title="Device",
        yaxis_title="Battery (%)",
    )
```

```
# Create CPU usage bar chart
cpu_fig                                    =
go.Figure(go.Bar(x=df_device_health['Device'],
y=df_device_health['CPU Usage (%)'], name='CPU
Usage (%)'))
    cpu_fig.update_layout(
        title="Device CPU Usage",
        xaxis_title="Device",
        yaxis_title="CPU Usage (%)",
    )

    return battery_fig, cpu_fig

if __name__ == '__main__':
    app.run_server(debug=True)
```

◆ Explanation:

- **Bar Charts**: The **battery status** and **CPU usage** are visualized using **bar charts** to show the health and performance of different IoT devices.
- **go.Bar()**: A simple bar chart that displays the metrics for each device.
- **Dash**: The app is an interactive dashboard for monitoring IoT devices, providing real-time insights into device health.

22.4 Summary and Next Steps

In this chapter, we:

- Worked with **sensor data** for real-time monitoring by visualizing temperature and humidity over time.
- Built a **real-time IoT data stream** dashboard using **Dash**, allowing users to filter and drill down into data.
- Created **device health monitoring dashboards**, visualizing battery levels and CPU usage for IoT devices.

Next Chapter: Advanced IoT Analytics and Predictive Modeling

In the next chapter, we will explore **advanced IoT analytics**, including **predictive maintenance**, **anomaly detection**, and **forecasting future device performance** using machine learning techniques.

◆ **Key Takeaway**: Visualizing **IoT data** using tools like **Dash** and **Plotly** allows businesses to monitor real-time data, track device health, and make informed decisions. **Interactive dashboards** enable real-time analysis, which is essential for effective decision-making in IoT environments.

CHAPTER 25

Visualizing Research Data

25.1 Visualizing Experimental and Scientific Research Data

Research data is at the heart of scientific discovery and experimentation. The ability to visualize experimental data effectively is crucial for drawing meaningful conclusions, communicating findings, and supporting hypothesis testing. Visualizations provide clarity and insight into complex datasets, making them easier to understand and interpret.

In this section, we will cover how to visualize different types of **scientific research data**, ranging from simple experimental results to more complex datasets involving multiple variables.

22.1.1 Visualizing Experimental Results

In many scientific fields, researchers use controlled experiments to test hypotheses. The results of these experiments are typically recorded in data tables and can be visualized through **bar charts**, **line graphs**, or **scatter plots**.

For example, if a researcher is studying the effect of **temperature** on **plant growth**, the data can be visualized in a **scatter plot** showing how the plant growth (in cm) changes as the temperature increases.

python

```
import plotly.graph_objects as go
import pandas as pd
import numpy as np

# Simulated experimental data for plant growth at
different temperatures
temperature = np.array([15, 20, 25, 30, 35, 40])
plant_growth = np.array([10, 12, 14, 16, 14, 10])

df_experiment = pd.DataFrame({
    'Temperature (°C)': temperature,
    'Plant Growth (cm)': plant_growth
})

# Create a scatter plot for the experimental
results
fig = go.Figure()

fig.add_trace(go.Scatter(x=df_experiment['Tempe
rature (°C)'],
                         y=df_experiment['Plant
Growth (cm)'],
```

```
                        mode='lines+markers',
name='Growth vs Temperature'))

fig.update_layout(
    title="Effect   of   Temperature   on   Plant
Growth",
    xaxis_title="Temperature (°C)",
    yaxis_title="Plant Growth (cm)"
)

fig.show()
```

◆ **Explanation**:

- The **scatter plot** is used to visualize the relationship between **temperature** and **plant growth**.
- `go.Scatter()`: The line and markers display the experiment's data points, allowing you to observe any patterns or trends.

22.2 Creating Charts and Plots for Hypothesis Testing

Hypothesis testing is an essential part of scientific research, helping to validate or reject hypotheses based on data. Visualizing the data involved in hypothesis tests allows researchers to better understand the distribution of their results and assess the validity of their conclusions.

22.2.1 Visualizing Distribution with Histograms

When performing hypothesis testing, it's important to visualize the distribution of data to check for **normality** or assess the **null hypothesis**. One way to do this is by creating a **histogram** to observe the frequency distribution of a dataset.

For instance, if a researcher is testing whether a new drug has a significant effect on blood pressure, a **histogram** can be used to show the distribution of **pre-treatment** and **post-treatment** blood pressure values.

```python
import plotly.express as px

# Simulated pre-treatment and post-treatment
blood pressure data
pre_treatment = np.random.normal(120, 15, 100)  #
Mean = 120, Std Dev = 15
post_treatment = np.random.normal(115, 12, 100)
# Mean = 115, Std Dev = 12

df_bp = pd.DataFrame({
```

```
    'Pre-Treatment': pre_treatment,
    'Post-Treatment': post_treatment
})


# Create a histogram to compare pre-treatment and
post-treatment blood pressure
fig  =  px.histogram(df_bp,  barmode="overlay",
histnorm='probability density',
                     title="Blood  Pressure  Before
and After Treatment",
                     labels={"value":        "Blood
Pressure (mmHg)"})
fig.update_traces(opacity=0.75)
fig.show()
```

◆ **Explanation**:

- **px.histogram()**: Creates a **histogram** to visualize the **distribution** of **blood pressure** values before and after treatment.
- **histnorm='probability density'**: Normalizes the histogram to show the **probability density** rather than raw frequencies.

22.2.2 Visualizing P-values and Confidence Intervals

Another key aspect of hypothesis testing is visualizing **p-values** and **confidence intervals**. Researchers often use **box**

plots to show the spread of data and determine whether the results of a hypothesis test fall within a certain **confidence interval**.

python

```python
# Simulated data for hypothesis testing
group1 = np.random.normal(50, 10, 100)   # Group
1 mean = 50
group2 = np.random.normal(55, 10, 100)   # Group
2 mean = 55

df_hypothesis = pd.DataFrame({
    'Group 1': group1,
    'Group 2': group2
})

# Create a box plot to visualize the difference
between two groups
fig   =   px.box(df_hypothesis,   points="all",
title="Comparison of Group 1 and Group 2",
            labels={'value':      'Measurement',
'variable': 'Group'})
fig.show()
```

♦ **Explanation**:

- **px.box()**: A **box plot** visualizes the **distribution** of the two groups, showing the **median, interquartile range (IQR)**, and **outliers**.
- This is helpful for determining if there is a significant difference between the groups, based on the data.

22.3 Visualizing Data Models and Simulations

In scientific research, **data models** and **simulations** are used to predict outcomes or explain complex phenomena. Visualization plays a key role in interpreting the results of these models, allowing researchers to explore their predictions and simulations interactively.

22.3.1 Visualizing Simulated Data with Scatter Plots

In many cases, simulations are used to predict outcomes under different conditions. For example, you might simulate the growth of a population over time based on a mathematical model, such as the **Logistic Growth Model.**

```python
# Simulate population growth using a logistic
growth model
```

```
time = np.arange(0, 100, 1)
K = 1000   # Carrying capacity
r = 0.05   # Growth rate
P0 = 10    # Initial population

population = K / (1 + ((K - P0) / P0) * np.exp(-
r * time))

# Create a scatter plot to visualize population
growth over time
fig    =    px.scatter(x=time,    y=population,
title="Simulated Population Growth",
                labels={'x':   'Time   (years)',
'y': 'Population'})
fig.show()
```

◆ Explanation:

- The **logistic growth model** is visualized using a **scatter plot** to show how the population grows over time, leveling off as it approaches the **carrying capacity (K)**.
- `np.exp()`: Exponentiation is used in the model to simulate growth over time.

22.3.2 Visualizing Regression Models and Predictions

Regression models are commonly used in research to predict the relationship between independent and dependent variables. Visualizing these models helps researchers understand the strength of the relationship and the significance of the prediction.

```python
from sklearn.linear_model import LinearRegression

# Simulated data for a linear regression model
X = np.random.rand(100, 1) * 10   # Random values for the independent variable
y = 2 * X + np.random.randn(100, 1) * 5   # Dependent variable with some noise

# Create a Linear Regression model
model = LinearRegression()
model.fit(X, y)

# Plot the regression line
fig = go.Figure()

fig.add_trace(go.Scatter(x=X.flatten(), y=y.flatten(), mode='markers', name='Data Points'))
fig.add_trace(go.Scatter(x=X.flatten(), y=model.predict(X).flatten(), mode='lines', name='Regression Line'))
```

```
fig.update_layout(
    title="Linear Regression Model",
    xaxis_title="Independent Variable",
    yaxis_title="Dependent Variable",
)

fig.show()
```

◆ Explanation:

- **Linear regression** is used to model the relationship between the independent variable **X** and the dependent variable **y**.
- `go.Scatter()`: This creates a **scatter plot** for the data points and a **line** for the regression model's prediction.

22.4 Summary and Next Steps

In this chapter, we:

- Visualized **experimental research data** using scatter plots and histograms to understand the relationship between different variables.
- Created **charts and plots for hypothesis testing**, such as visualizing **p-values**, **confidence intervals**, and **distributions**.

- Visualized **data models and simulations**, including population growth models and regression analysis, to predict and explain real-world phenomena.

Next Chapter: Advanced Research Data Analytics with Machine Learning

In the next chapter, we will explore **advanced techniques** in **research data analysis**, including the use of **machine learning models** to detect patterns, predict outcomes, and perform complex analyses on research datasets.

◆ **Key Takeaway**: Visualizing **research data** is essential for making sense of experimental results, performing hypothesis testing, and interpreting complex data models. Tools like **Plotly** and **Dash** help researchers create clear, interactive visualizations that facilitate deeper insights and more informed decision-making. 🚀

PART 6

BEST PRACTICES AND FUTURE DIRECTIONS

CHAPTER 26

Best Practices for Data Visualization

Data visualization is more than just presenting charts and graphs; it's about effectively conveying insights and enabling decision-making. As a data scientist or analyst, your goal is to create clear, engaging, and insightful visualizations that not only show data but also **tell a story**. In this chapter, we'll discuss the **best practices** for designing **effective visualizations**, the **common pitfalls** to avoid, and how to ensure your visualizations **tell a compelling story**.

26.1 Guidelines for Creating Clear, Insightful, and Effective Visualizations

When designing data visualizations, you must ensure that they are both **informative** and **easily understood** by your audience. Here are some best practices for creating effective charts and graphs:

26.1.1 Choose the Right Type of Visualization

Selecting the right type of chart or graph is key to effectively communicating your data. The **type of visualization** you

299

choose should match the message you want to convey. Here are some common chart types and when to use them:

- **Bar Chart**: Best for comparing categories, such as **sales by region** or **performance by department**.
- **Line Chart**: Great for showing **trends over time**, such as **stock prices, temperature changes**, or **website traffic**.
- **Pie Chart**: Suitable for showing **proportional data** or parts of a whole, such as **market share** or **survey responses**.
- **Scatter Plot**: Used to visualize **correlations** between two variables, such as **height vs. weight** or **advertising spend vs. sales**.
- **Heatmap**: Ideal for visualizing **density** or **intensity**, such as **customer behavior** or **website engagement** across different days of the week.

26.1.2 Keep It Simple and Avoid Clutter

Clarity is key in data visualization. Avoid overcrowding your charts with unnecessary elements like **3D effects, excessive text**, or **unneeded gridlines**. The goal is to highlight the **key message** in the simplest way possible.

- Use **minimalist design** with clear **axis labels, titles**, and **legends**.

- Keep the **color palette** simple and consistent. Too many colors can overwhelm the viewer and distract from the key insights.
- Avoid **chartjunk**—visual elements that don't add value to the story, such as **extraneous borders, background images**, or unnecessary decorations.

26.1.3 Provide Context

Your visualizations should include sufficient context so that viewers can easily interpret the data. This can be achieved through:

- **Labels**: Ensure all axes, data points, and legend items are clearly labeled.
- **Annotations**: Use annotations to highlight important data points, trends, or outliers that the audience should pay attention to.
- **Titles and Descriptions**: Include clear titles and brief descriptions to explain the data and its significance.

26.2 Common Pitfalls and How to Avoid Them

While designing visualizations, there are several common mistakes to watch out for that can undermine the clarity and effectiveness of your charts:

26.2.1 Misleading Visualizations

A common pitfall is using visualizations that **mislead** the audience. Some common techniques that can distort the data include:

- **Manipulating the Y-axis**: Avoid truncating the Y-axis or using a **non-zero baseline** for bar charts, as this can exaggerate differences.

  Example:

    o   A bar chart that starts from **100** rather than **0** can make small differences appear much larger than they really are.

- **3D Charts**: **3D charts** (like **3D bar charts** or **scatter plots**) may look visually appealing, but they often make it difficult to accurately assess the data and can distort perspectives.

- **Pie Charts with Too Many Segments**: While pie charts are good for showing proportions, they can become hard to read if there are too many segments.

Use them for **few categories** and avoid using them for more than 6-8 categories.

26.2.2 Overcomplicating Visualizations

Visualizations should focus on **clarity** and **simplicity**, not complexity. Overcomplicating the visualization with too many data series, fancy chart types, or excessive decoration can confuse the viewer.

- Stick to **one key message** per chart.
- Avoid overloading the chart with too many data points or variables.

26.2.3 Ignoring Audience Needs

When creating a visualization, always consider your audience's **level of expertise** and **specific needs**. For example, a **business executive** may need a high-level dashboard with clear **KPIs**, while a **data scientist** may prefer a detailed scatter plot with multiple variables.

- **Tailor the visualization** to your audience's background and requirements.
- Use **clear labeling** and **contextual information** to ensure that your visualization is understandable to your target audience.

26.3 Making Sure Your Visualizations Tell a Story

A great data visualization doesn't just present data; it **tells a story**. The purpose of data visualization is to guide the viewer to an **insightful conclusion**, and this can be achieved by effectively using the elements of **data storytelling**.

26.3.1 Start with the Key Message

The first step in creating a compelling visualization is to decide on the **key message** you want to communicate. Every visualization should be focused on **one main takeaway**, whether it's understanding **trends over time**, **comparing categories**, or **identifying outliers**.

- Ask yourself: What is the **question** this visualization is trying to answer?
- Focus on presenting the data in a way that makes the answer to that question **immediately clear**.

26.3.2 Use Visual Elements to Guide the Viewer

Just like a story, a good visualization has a **beginning**, **middle**, and **end**. Use visual elements to guide the viewer through the data:

- **Titles and Labels**: Use **titles** to introduce the key message and **labels** to guide the viewer's eye to important data points.
- **Color and Size**: Use color and size to highlight important elements and draw attention to key insights, like **outliers** or **trends**.
- **Annotations**: Add **annotations** to explain data points or trends and provide context for the viewer.

26.3.3 Incorporate Interactivity

Interactivity allows the viewer to engage with the data and explore different facets of the visualization. Tools like **Dash** and **Plotly** can be used to build interactive visualizations where users can:

- Filter data (e.g., by date range, category, or region).
- Hover over data points to get more information (e.g., exact values).
- Zoom in to focus on a specific area of the chart.

Interactivity helps the viewer **explore** the data on their own, making it a more **personalized experience** and uncovering deeper insights.

26.4 Summary and Best Practices Recap

In this chapter, we:

- Discussed the **best practices** for creating effective and insightful visualizations, including choosing the right chart type, maintaining simplicity, and providing sufficient context.
- Identified **common pitfalls** like misleading visualizations and overcomplicating charts, and provided tips on how to avoid them.
- Emphasized the importance of **storytelling** in data visualization, making sure that each chart or graph communicates a clear and compelling message.

Next Chapter: Future Directions in Data Visualization

As we look ahead, data visualization is rapidly evolving. In the next chapter, we will explore the **future of data visualization** in fields such as **augmented reality**, **AI-driven visualizations**, and **real-time interactive dashboards**, as well as how emerging technologies are transforming how we analyze and present data.

♦ **Key Takeaway**: **Effective data visualization** goes beyond simply plotting data—it's about conveying insights clearly and engagingly. By following best practices and focusing on storytelling, you can create visualizations that not only inform but also inspire action and deeper understanding. 🚀

CHAPTER 27

The Future of Data Visualization

27.1 Emerging Trends in Data Visualization Tools and Libraries

The field of data visualization is rapidly evolving, with new tools and technologies making it easier to analyze, interpret, and communicate data. As businesses, researchers, and individuals generate more complex datasets, the demand for more **interactive**, **dynamic**, and **insightful** visualizations continues to grow. Let's explore some of the emerging trends in the world of data visualization.

27.1.1 AI-Driven Visualization Tools

As data becomes increasingly complex, traditional static charts are no longer enough. Tools are incorporating **artificial intelligence (AI)** to automatically generate visualizations that are tailored to the specific characteristics of the data. These AI-driven tools can help users:

- Automatically **identify patterns** in data.

- Recommend the **best visualization types** based on the nature of the data.

- Predict trends or anomalies using **machine learning algorithms** and present them in easily interpretable visual formats.

For example, **Tableau** and **Power BI** have integrated **AI-driven analytics** that automatically suggest charts based on data input, making it easier for users to generate insights quickly without having to manually choose visualization types.

27.1.2 Real-Time Data Visualization

Real-time data visualization is becoming increasingly important as industries like **finance, healthcare**, and **IoT** rely on immediate insights from constantly changing data. Tools and libraries are evolving to handle **streaming data** and deliver **live updates**.

- **Dash** and **Plotly** are already leaders in this field, offering the ability to create **interactive dashboards** that update in real time, allowing users to monitor data streams and receive insights as they happen.

- The rise of **cloud computing** is facilitating the scalability and speed required for real-time visualizations, allowing organizations to manage massive datasets without delay.

27.1.3 Immersive and 3D Visualizations

The integration of **virtual reality (VR)** and **augmented reality (AR)** is taking data visualization to the next level, allowing users to interact with data in 3D environments.

- **3D visualizations** allow users to explore multidimensional data, providing deeper insights and enabling **better decision-making**. For instance, **scientific researchers** can use 3D models to represent data from simulations or experiments in a more immersive way.
- Tools such as **Unity** and **Three.js** are paving the way for creating interactive 3D data visualizations, where users can manipulate models, zoom in on particular areas, and gain a better understanding of complex data sets.

27.2 Integrating AI and Machine Learning with Visualizations

As the role of **artificial intelligence (AI)** and **machine learning (ML)** continues to expand, their integration into data visualization tools offers exciting possibilities. AI and ML can help uncover insights, automate processes, and enhance decision-making by adding predictive and diagnostic capabilities to visualizations.

27.2.1 Predictive Visualizations

AI and ML models can now be used to predict future trends based on historical data. These predictions can be visualized in real-time, allowing businesses and organizations to make proactive decisions.

For example:

- **Time-series forecasting** using **machine learning models** such as **ARIMA** or **prophet** can be visualized using **line charts** that show predicted future values alongside actual historical data.
- **Anomaly detection** models can highlight **outliers** in real-time visualizations, drawing attention to unexpected events or potential risks.

27.2.2 Automating Insights

Machine learning algorithms can automatically **analyze data** and suggest insights without requiring human intervention. For example, AI tools can **identify patterns** in large datasets and **recommend visualizations** to represent those patterns.

- **Deep learning models** could analyze unstructured data (like images or text) and provide insights that can be visualized, such as recognizing objects in satellite imagery or sentiment analysis of social media posts.
- **Natural Language Processing (NLP)** tools, integrated with data visualization, could allow users to ask questions in plain language, and the AI would generate the appropriate visualization. For instance, "What were the peak sales days last month?" could prompt the system to create a bar chart showing the highest sales days.

27.2.3 Interactive AI Models in Dashboards

AI can also enhance **interactive dashboards** by dynamically adjusting visualizations based on user inputs. As users filter or drill down into data, AI models can adjust to reveal new insights. This kind of intelligent interaction enables more personalized and useful data exploration.

27.3 The Role of Interactivity in the Future of Data Analysis

Interactivity is a key feature that allows users to explore data, drill down into specific areas, and uncover new insights on the fly. As data becomes more complex, **interactive visualizations** will play a crucial role in how we analyze and interpret information. Let's explore the role of interactivity in the future of data analysis.

27.3.1 Interactive Dashboards

Interactive dashboards allow users to engage with data through **filters, drop-down menus, sliders**, and **hover-over interactions**. These elements empower users to explore data from different perspectives, making it easier to draw conclusions and make data-driven decisions.

- **Plotly Dash** and **Streamlit** are widely used for creating **real-time, interactive dashboards**.
- These platforms allow you to build **customized data visualizations** that update dynamically based on user inputs. This is especially useful for monitoring business metrics, real-time analytics, and **IoT data**.

27.3.2 Drill-Down Capabilities

Drill-down features let users start with a high-level overview and then "drill down" into more granular details as needed.

This interactive capability is essential for analyzing **large datasets**, where the user can focus on specific categories or time periods.

For example:

- A business dashboard displaying overall **sales** might allow the user to drill down into specific **regions, product categories**, or **time frames** to explore more detailed performance metrics.
- **Hierarchical visualizations**, such as **sunburst charts** or **treemaps**, make it easy to visualize hierarchical data structures while enabling users to interactively zoom into specific subcategories.

27.3.3 Interactive Machine Learning Visualizations

In the context of **machine learning**, interactive visualizations allow users to **explore model predictions** and understand model performance better.

- **Model evaluation** can be made interactive by displaying **confusion matrices, ROC curves**, and **precision-recall curves** in an interactive format, allowing users to explore how different metrics change with different model parameters.

- **Feature importance** visualizations, where users can hover over or click on features to see how they contribute to a model's predictions, can help users understand the driving factors behind the model.

27.3.4 Storytelling Through Data

Interactive visualizations not only allow users to explore data but also help **tell a story**. By guiding users through a series of steps, showing relevant data points, and allowing interaction with the visualizations, you can **narrate a data story** that highlights key insights.

- **Flowcharts**, **timelines**, and **progress indicators** help users understand the sequence of events or changes in data over time.
- **Annotations** and **tooltips** can be added to charts to provide context or highlight significant findings, making the data narrative more engaging and insightful.

27.4 Summary and Conclusion

In this chapter, we explored the future of **data visualization** and how emerging trends, the integration of **AI and**

machine learning, and the rise of **interactive tools** will transform how we analyze and interpret data:

- **AI-driven tools** are automating insights and helping users choose the best visualizations based on their data.
- **Real-time data visualization** is becoming essential for industries that require instant feedback, such as **finance**, **healthcare**, and **IoT**.
- **Machine learning models** are being integrated into visualizations, helping users make predictions, detect anomalies, and improve decision-making.
- **Interactivity** in dashboards and visualizations is empowering users to drill down into data, explore insights, and gain a deeper understanding of complex datasets.

As technology continues to evolve, data visualization will become more intuitive, dynamic, and automated, helping users unlock new insights and make data-driven decisions faster than ever before.

Next Chapter: The Role of Artificial Intelligence in Data Science

In the next chapter, we will dive deeper into the role of **artificial intelligence** in **data science**, exploring how AI is transforming data collection, analysis, and visualization across industries.

◆ **Key Takeaway**: The future of data visualization is bright, with **AI**, **machine learning**, and **interactivity** playing pivotal roles in how we analyze and interpret data. By staying ahead of these trends, businesses can make more informed decisions and unlock deeper insights.

www.ingramcontent.com/pod-product-compliance
Lightning Source LLC
LaVergne TN
LVHW051432050326
832903LV00030BD/3044